Published in Great Britain by
L.R. Price Publications Ltd, 2022
27 Old Gloucester Street,
London, WC1N 3AX
www.lrpricepublications.com

ISBN: 9781739805272

FINDING THE GOOD LIFE AS A SWALEADER

Effective Leadership in Our New World

Zachary Paul Hoffman

"Mishaps are like knives, that either serve us or cut us, as we grasp them by the blade or the handle."

James Russell Lowell.

"I don't know what my future holds, but I do know who holds my future."

Tim Tebow.

DEDICATION

This book is dedicated to my mom and dad, all the young players I've had the pleasure of mentoring and my coaches, teammates and friends all across Europe, who helped, supported and brought me so much joy throughout the years. Your impact on my life will never be forgotten.

Special thanks to Coach Roberto Cestari, Coach Aaron Mitchell, Coach Tony Simmons, Coach Dan Miles, Coach Andy Pröller, Mr. Nicola Salvi, Georg Weigl, Amir Pirkhadem, Laura Sophia Hummel, the Hummel Family and my good friend Jason Cass.

Vorrei ringraziare il mio grande amici Frank Visone, Al Fenderico. Anche, Coach Amedeo Carpentieri, Coach Mimo Gentile e le loro bellissime famiglie, per tutto quello che hanno fatto, per me durante il mio periodo a Napoli. Ti voglio bene a tutti e non ti dimenticherò mai...

CONTENTS

PREFACE

It was February 2015, and I was enjoying my fourth season playing American football abroad. A few members of my team and our coach had gathered in my small flat on the outskirts of Naples, Italy, for pizza and Peroni beer after 5 p.m. practice. It was a surprisingly warm evening, and I remember the high-pitched voices of children playing soccer in the narrow alley below. My fellow American coach and I sat on the sofa enjoying a glass of wine, while we discussed our experience living abroad.

He had been playing and coaching outside the United States for fifteen years, and had been to just about every country in the world. I, on the other hand, was simply a young man with no idea about what I would do with my life outside of sports, and I told him as much, when he asked about my plans after my football career ended.

My coach bit his lip, shook his head and said the words that have helped shape the man I've become: "Zach, you need to start taking leadership of your own life. Football is great while it's here, but it won't last forever; don't fall into the trap."

I remember feeling a sudden rush of anxiety and my heartbeat increase. That night, I lay in bed and asked myself: "What did he actually mean by 'taking leadership of my life'? What was 'the trap' he was talking about?" I already assumed I was a great leader, who was living a fulfilling life. I finally fell asleep without answers.

But when I woke up the next morning it hit me. What had defined my entire existence since I was five years old was going to come to an end sooner than I imagined. I had no identity outside of sports and athletics. I took pride in being a quarterback and leader of my football team, but I had failed to take leadership of my future.

My coach's words opened my eyes, and I knew I had to make some changes and redefine what true leadership was. Little did I know that I would have a long and challenging road ahead.

REALIZATION: LEADERSHIP ISN'T ENOUGH

A lot of people lay claim to the title of "leader" simply because it makes them seem qualified for a more prestigious position. However, many fail to understand how effective leadership works – *effective* being the operative word. In my personal experience, I have seen people hold leadership positions because they were academically qualified, but who lacked the skill of effective leadership required to make an impact in that role.

Throughout this book, you will see terms like *developing, aspiring* and *effective leadership*. The reason I don't use the word "leadership" alone is simply because that doesn't always convey its full meaning and true purpose. The unfortunate reality is that there are a number of people occupying various leadership roles who are ineffective and flawed in their leadership methods. The purpose of this book is to help aspiring, morally driven leaders realize, grow and develop their leadership capabilities, as it relates to an ever-changing business culture.

You will also see the acronym "SWAL" throughout this book, which means "Swiss Army Leadership". Just as a Swiss Army knife is diverse in its functionality, the same must also be true for aspiring leaders in modern society. The SWAL concept is the basis for this book, and is a model I have developed from my ten years of living and working in six different countries.

What I have learned more than anything is that people are different. It sounds like a simple realization, but it is crucial to effective leadership. SWAL requires one to dig deeper, and not just deal with people at surface level. In order to truly earn one's respect and trust, it is vital that we understand the importance of using our social skills, to reach each individual in a group. The SWAL concept is my solution to achieving effective, modern-day leadership by adapting these social skills and using them, to leave a legacy and acquire a sense of fulfilment. Implementing the SWAL model will help heighten one's awareness of the different personalities and motivating factors present within society.

As I mentioned earlier, there is a huge difference between effective leadership and mere leadership. The good news is that effective leadership can be developed. There is a popular saying that "leaders are born, not made" – well, from my experience, I strongly disagree; effective leaders can be developed! I am living proof of this fact.

Now, you may wonder who I am to make such a bold claim. While I am not a famous athlete like LeBron James, a billionaire C.E.O. like Mark Zuckerberg, or a well-known speaker like Tony Robbins, I am a young man who has lived a fulfilling and eventful life. From the age of eighteen, I have had the rare privilege of being in various leadership roles in six different countries. I accepted the challenge to effectively lead people from all walks of life, from the United States to Poland, France, Germany, Italy and Austria, and I have had the opportunity to see and experience life in its different forms. My experiences have been amazingly beautiful, with a fair share of disheartening ones. Through my mistakes and my triumphs, I have realized how important effective leadership is, in regard to personal and collective success, as well as emotional fulfilment.

In the end, there is no doubt that I have been blessed, as what I do is something I never could have imagined, growing up in a tiny, rural town in Western Pennsylvania. My experiences have inspired me to help people to become more effective leaders in all aspects of their lives, and understand that they can change their life and mentality for the better, if they make the commitment and take action! I have the experience to prove that the Swiss Army Leadership concept is a model for success, for everyone, from the most prominent businessperson to the parent coaching their son's or daughter's youth soccer team.

In this book, I will also share personal experiences which I hope will prove to you the effectiveness of SWAL. It is my hope that, at the end, you will have gained a new perspective on what effective modern-day leadership looks like.

There is no doubt that our society needs to move away from the ineffectiveness of past methods, and move forward into developing quality, morally driven leaders. These are the people who will eventually lay the path to bringing our broken society back together again. I strongly believe that societal ills such as racism, the love of money, selfishness, etc. can be directly traced to a lack of effective leadership.

So, let's dive into what it means to be a SWALeader...

GETTING ON POINT: DEFINING EFFECTIVE LEADERSHIP

If you Google the word "leadership", you will come across a variety of definitions. Oftentimes, these definitions are quite bland and leave one to assume that leadership is a walk in the park. In my opinion, this kind of assumption is the main reason for a lot of the structural issues we face today, in life and business. To my surprise, even credible dictionaries like Merriam-Webster define leadership in such simple terms as:

"the office or position of..."
"capacity to lead..."
"the act or an instance of leading..."

Unfortunately, it seems that not even society can concretely define leadership. It is amazing to me that we cannot give proper definition to a concept which is so vital to society's success and output. Another part of the problem is that our society tends to define leadership solely based on position title or job description, while disregarding the skillset or abilities needed to actually carry out the *responsibilities* of leadership. The reality is, even though someone may have a well-respected job title, that doesn't always mean that he or she possesses the characteristics to lead effectively. Maybe he or she went to a great university, performed well academically, paid his dues or utilized his network in order to ascend the corporate hierarchy, or is even a genius and proven expert in his field, however, if he or she cannot properly connect to, inspire and motivate those under his leadership, he is already set up for failure.

Some people may call this the difference between so-called "street-smarts" (our personal foundation and social skills) and "book-smarts" (academic knowledge). The question is: which is more important? From my experience, society dictates that it is book-smarts. While book-smarts certainly play a huge role in defining one's credibility, without the necessary street-smarts, leaders will have little chance of prolonged success. However, as a result of society placing such a high premium on a college diploma, many people find their way into these leadership positions due to their book-smarts. The problem with this is that acquiring knowledge via countless hours of reading textbooks and studying for exams has little to zero impact on developing effective leadership skills.

Why is that? Because effective leadership involves social interaction – and by "social interaction" I don't mean going out drinking with your friends at the weekends. Effective interaction is how well one who possesses knowledge can express it, in such a way that others can understand and learn from it. Just because a person is highly educated, doesn't necessarily mean that he or she possesses the capability to effectively lead others.

While street-smarts and book-smarts are totally different, they go hand in hand when it comes to effective leadership. Without some fundamental knowledge, it is impossible to gain the credibility that is needed to enter a leadership role in the first place (especially in the corporate world). On the other hand, without a solid personal foundation and social skills, it really doesn't matter how much knowledge you may have; it won't make any difference if you're not able to express it in a way that others can understand.

KNOWLEDGE IS POWER? NOT SO FAST

We have all heard the phrase "knowledge is power". While I believe this statement to have a lot of truth to it, as far as personal development and awareness goes, I also believe it is flawed in relation to effective leadership. In my experience, I have found that many consider power and leadership in the same light. In my opinion, this saying cannot be adopted literally, with regards to effective leadership.

Power is often associated with those who withhold and/or acquire large amounts of money. For the sake of morality, let's just assume that this money was acquired in an ethical way; this means it took financial knowledge and the ability to make smart money decisions to earn it. This is clearly a strategy others would be inclined to follow, and therefore this wealthy person may be seen as an effective leader, solely based on his financial literacy and the fact that he has money; companies may then look at his results and want to put him in a leadership role. However, who is to say that this person:

- has the willingness to share his knowledge;
- has the ability to express it in a way others will understand;
- has the social skills needed to reach others and inspire them to follow?

I am sure we all know someone like that – maybe a teacher or a boss in the workplace. There is an excessive number of very successful, wealthy, knowledgeable people out there, who simply do not have the ability to connect with people and express their knowledge in a way that others can understand. The point is this: while it often acquires someone in a leadership position, knowledge alone doesn't equate to effective leadership.

In simpler terms, we can break this concept down into an equation:

General societal equation:

Knowledge = power (leadership).

SWAL's equation:

Knowledge + personal foundation + social skills = power (effective leadership).

LET'S GET PHYSICAL: WHEN GREAT TALENT AND POOR LEADERSHIP COLLIDE

Another example of society's flawed ideas about leadership can be seen in professional sports, particularly American football. I must mention that I will be using a number of sports-related terms in this book; I grew up participating in all types of sports, then subsequently played professional football in Europe. Even if you have never played sports, just realize that what goes on in sports pretty much sums up what goes on in everyday life and business.

In the game of football, the quarterback's position is said to be the one which requires the most leadership skills. This is the reason most teams are frantic in their search for a quarterback with the "it" factor, yet when they are asked what that "it" is, they are unable to give a definitive answer. While all quarterbacks at the professional level have excellent talent and ability to perform on the field, few possess the maturity needed for long-term success in areas such as effectively leading their team and making sacrifices, on and off the field, which other players aren't able to make. Some famous examples are Johnny "Football" Manziel, Ryan Leaf and Todd Marinovich. I'm not trying to criticize these players, and it is clear that they have learned from their mistakes, but it proves that a person's talent can make society blind to their faulty foundations. There is no doubt that talent is very important, but it can only get you so far; when it collides with poor leadership, it becomes a recipe for disaster. Examples to buttress this point are scattered throughout history.

Practically everyone on the planet has heard about the Watergate scandal, during the presidency of Richard Nixon. He had a good reputation as a former lieutenant commander; he was elected to the House of Representatives and had solid foreign policies; clearly, he had the talent and experience that helped him become president of the United States, but his actions – to become known as the "Watergate scandal" – made him the first and only president in U.S. history to resign from the position. This, then, begs the question: is talent the most important factor in effective leadership? According to society, the answer is an overwhelming yes. However, the fact of the matter is, more often than not, that great talent blinds one to the bigger picture. SWALeaders must not fall into the trap of focusing on physical talent as the basis for sustained leadership, and becoming blinded to the big picture.

ARE YOU WILLING? EFFECTIVE LEADERSHIP REQUIRES SACRIFICE

We have a great deal of self-proclaimed leaders in today's world. Does that mean that they are all effective? Well, answering "yes" to this rhetorical question would be like saying that everyone who goes to the gym is a fitness model, which simply isn't true; not everyone has the willpower to put in the hard work necessary to develop a six-pack! Most people are fine with their $20 per month membership, and the 30-minute workouts three days a week, while socializing with other members. Sure, we would all like to have the body of a fitness model, but the sacrifice needed to get there is too great, or simply not worth the time and effort for most people. But this doesn't mean one can't commit to the process of becoming a fitness model, if one truly wants to. The process of becoming an effective leader isn't any different.

In three words, effective leaders sacrifice. This means giving up immediate pleasures for long-term results. For example, a fitness model sacrifices the immediate and brief pleasure of eating ice cream or a chocolate bar, in order to maintain her figure and long-term career success. In the same vein, effective leaders must also let go of things or character traits which will cause them to lose credibility. When a person in a leadership role decides to drink too much at the weekend, this is a decision to indulge in short-term pleasure. What if it just so happens that, while he is at the club, an acquaintance posts a picture of him on his social media timeline with one eye half-closed, a crooked smile and a plastic cup filled with beer in his hand; this photo is then seen by his employees and/or managers, and leads to tension, embarrassment and a lack of trust within the organization. It is not uncommon to find managers at any level who are unwilling to give up their status quo and make this sacrifice, because most people just want to have the title of "leader" without actually living it.

I have come to learn that effective leadership is a lifestyle which requires you to shift your focus from short-term pleasure to long-term results. Those who claim the title of "leader", without sacrificing to live like one, are simply in it for themselves, and the attention which comes with the position. This kind of person will have a hard time sustaining credibility because, eventually, his or her true motives will be exposed. It is important to remember that titles don't always mean that someone is an effective leader; prestigious job titles, fame, power and money simply expose people for who they really are, and it is only a matter of time before they self-sabotage.

HUMBLE YOURSELF: IT'S OKAY TO FOLLOW

The idea of being a follower is not a popular one; for some reason, it seems low-level, disrespectful and insulting. In reality, though, there is no shame in following an effective leader.

Everyone has the innate ability to become an effective leader, but not everyone has the will or desire to lead effectively. In other words, not everyone can effectively lead based on his situation, morals and values; there are few who will commit to making the sacrifice for a greater cause. I'm not saying that it's impossible; I simply mean that everyone's situation is different, and oftentimes the temptations/weight of outside forces are too powerful for someone to commit to becoming an effective leader, at any particular time. In this case, there is no shame in humbling oneself, and following capable people who can lead you in the right direction.

I am a perfect example. Several times, I desired to be in leadership roles, based on my experience and ego, but I was incapable of leading with success at that time. One such situation was when I was offered the position of Head Coach for a youth football team in Italy. Deep down, I knew that my life circumstances at that time would not allow me to lead effectively, so I opted to be an assistant coach, because I knew that the man who would be chosen for the job in my place was in a better position to lead effectively. It turned out that he was just the kind of leader that the players and even I myself needed. What I learned from this is that being under the guidance of an effective leader puts you in a position to learn and be better prepared for your next leadership opportunity.

We can't let our egos get in the way of our current reality, and I believe this is especially true in politics and business. People can get so used to being in a position of power and control that they sometimes make decisions based on their ego and emotions, rather than logic and the best interest of their employees/followers. In simpler terms, they are often guilty of being selfish. Effective leaders must be able to let go of the lust for personal success, for the sake of the group which follows them; in other words, put the best interest of the followers first. This is hard to do, because humans are selfish by nature, but it is possible, because beneath the selfishness exist the qualities of compassion and care for others. The most authentic example of these qualities are shown when a mother cares for and nurtures her children – we will take a closer look at this example later on.

The bottom line is that we, as aspiring leaders, have to understand the importance of choosing selflessness over selfishness and, in my opinion, this is one of the major internal struggles faced in the process of becoming an effective leader. There are always two voices in our heads: one tells us to be selfish and the other tells us to be selfless. For example, if you happen to find a valuable item, such as a diamond ring, on the ground, you will most likely struggle with the choice of reporting it to the authorities or keeping it for yourself. What you decide to do will be based on the morals and values in which you are rooted.

THE SWALIFE: THE IDEA BEHIND SWISS ARMY LEADERSHIP

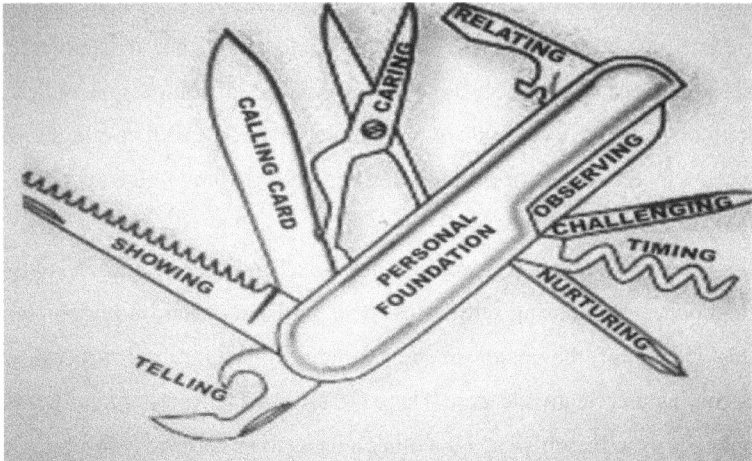

From my experience, I've come to the realization that one of the biggest mistakes in business and personal relationships is assumption. It is amazing to me how people still make assumptions, even when the stakes are high. This is a huge reason why many relationships (personal and business) fail, or never develop in the first place; a lot of amazing opportunities are lost, simply because of stubbornness and an unwillingness to adapt.

But there is a better way.

I developed a desire to help people regain some of these lost opportunities and help shape a better future, and I believe this can be accomplished by adjusting standardized leadership norms to take on a more adaptable, hybrid approach. Through the lens of my experiences abroad, I see that intercultural competence and the development of strong people skills are essential to effective leadership and sustained success.

This led me to develop the analogy of using a Swiss Army knife as a representation of how people can appropriately adapt and enhance their leadership skills, to best serve modern-day society. This adaptation requires a process which abandons much of what we have learned in the past. As a SWALeader, one must commit to becoming an expert in understanding, acceptance, people skills and selflessness. These qualities are quite scarce amongst the general population, and the purpose of SWAL is to develop these qualities and adapt them to specific individuals, situations and cultures all over the world. Just like a Swiss Army knife is diverse in the tasks it can perform, so should our leadership style be diverse enough to meet the needs of each individual or group. One specific leadership style will not work for everyone; the way one person may be inspired or motivated would probably be different from another person – an effective leader must be able to recognize this and adapt. People come from diverse backgrounds, have different personality traits and hold varied belief systems – this is particularly true when operating in an international environment.

We have all heard the saying: *"Treat others in the way you want to be treated."* I believe that this widely applied concept has been misinterpreted, because the way one person wants to be treated is, more often than not, different from the way the next person prefers to be treated. In his book *How to Win Friends and Influence People*, Dale Carnegie confirms this ideology by saying: *"treat others the way they want to be treated."* Treating others the way they want to be treated implies that you take the time to understand each individual (the same way you would like to be understood), in order to treat them the best way possible, based on their personality and motivations. We need to stop making assumptions about others based on our own personal preferences; understand that each person is different and should be treated as such.

Generalized assumptions made by someone in a leadership role only lead to misunderstandings, tension, a lack of respect and divisiveness.

A SWALeader is an all-leader. We must understand the importance of earning the respect of each individual for whom we are responsible. While this definitely takes extra time and effort, it is crucial for sustained success, fulfilment and legacy.

It is not possible for everyone to like you or your style of leadership, but I have come to realize that the attention to detail which comes with adopting the SWAL concept makes that the exception, not the rule. The secret is choosing to recreate ourselves and our personal foundation, by adapting the necessary tools and traits.

The idea of SWAL is to reach and relate to the people who matter in your life. These people are the ones who play a pivotal role in your life's legacy; they are your colleagues, friends, potential business partners, or people you want to help. I want to make one point clear here: SWAL doesn't account for haters or trolls, because they don't have any power over you; the people who matter, in regard to your goals, are the ones who must be your allies. This means we must adapt our strategy to make room for each individual who matters to us.

The argument against SWAL may sound something like this: *"I like who I am; I don't have to adjust for anybody; I don't care if people like me or not; in fact, I am a successful leader the way I am!"* If this is truly your mindset, you are living in the past and will not enjoy sustained success in a leadership role in today's world. We can complain or we can choose to improve and adapt our people skills, while developing a more selfless mindset, in order to make a positive and transformational impact on society. This is essentially what SWAL is: a choice.

In the midst of all the negativity the world has had to deal with in 2020, we live in a time of great opportunity; the world is more accessible than it ever has been. There is no doubt that the world has changed dramatically in the last twenty years, and it will continue to do so; it therefore surprises me that, in spite of all the changes the world has undergone, the school system still teaches the same coursework which was taught to our parents and grandparents. This is unhelpful, because the information is outdated and ineffective for modern, real-world encounters.

Without awareness, acceptance, tolerance and adaptability, there will be tension, divisiveness and hatred toward those who don't look or think like we do. This means that, in order to make an impact in a leadership role, we need to adapt. My experiences have shown me that aspiring leaders need to grasp the concept of SWAL, now more than ever, in order to be effective.

One morning in January, I realized that I was out of coffee. I had a long day ahead of me and knew I would need the caffeine boost, so I put on my boots and jacket, and made the trip to the local grocery store down the street. However, I didn't check the store's opening hours before leaving my home, so when I arrived at the store I had to wait an extra ten minutes. There was an older man in his mid- to late-sixties waiting, as well. For the first few minutes we didn't speak at all, and I hoped he wouldn't speak to me, because I had a hard time understanding the Salzburg German dialect that a lot of the older people used. After about five minutes, he said: "Hey, junger Mann, weißt du wie spät es ist?" *("Hey, young man, do you know what time it is?")* Thankfully, I could understand him, so I glanced at my phone and told him the time. He recognized my accent and immediately asked: "Von woher kommst du?" *("Where are you from?")* I told him I was American and part Italian. He smiled in approval and asked: "Bist du Katholisch?" *("Are you Catholic?")* Not wanting to get into a deep conversation with him, I simply nodded. He smiled again and pointed inside the grocery store, directing my attention to a young lady wearing a headscarf, who was sweeping the floor: "Siehst du diese Frau, junger Mann? Sie kommt aus der Turkei. Wir mussen aufpassen; weil diese Leute gefahrlich sind. Sie wollen uns nicht hier." *("You see this woman, young man? She comes from Turkey. These people are dangerous; we have to be careful. These types of people don't want us around)"*.

I took a closer look at this young girl, who was maybe 5 feet 2 inches tall, and probably weighed no more than ninety pounds. Thinking of her as dangerous made me chuckle. Obviously, I knew he didn't mean this lady in particular, but Middle Easterners in general. It was clear that his prior questions were simply a fishing expedition, to see how similar we were, and it didn't hurt that my skin was the same color as his; in fact, apart from my accent, I could easily pass for an Austrian guy. The gentleman made some more small talk, asking about my family and so on; I guess I had gained his approval, because he was very kind to me. He told me he used to be a schoolteacher, and even pulled out his wallet to proudly show me a picture of his grandchildren.

I couldn't get that conversation out of my mind. That man clearly had issues with foreigners and people who were different from him, and he was raised to think that way. I thought about his children, grandchildren and all the students he taught over the course of his career, and wondered whether they all thought the same way. My thoughts moved to my home country, and the divisiveness which is still prevalent today, and I realized that this is not an Austrian or American problem alone, but a global one; prejudice is passed down from generation to generation. I am not saying that we aren't becoming more open to acceptance and change, but more work needs to be done if we're going to reach our full potential. Issues which need to be addressed include racial tension; a lack of understanding of people from other cultures; an inability to interact or communicate with others, based on differing beliefs; and an unwillingness to accept and learn from people of different backgrounds.

It is our job as adults to groom the leaders of the future, and we must break away from outdated ideologies and negative belief systems, which are not only ineffective, but harmful as well.

The totalitarian model of leadership is no longer effective. Someone who uses the power of their job title as an excuse to order people around while doing nothing is completely futile, and will bring about disastrous outcomes in today's world, yet this strategy was once seen as effective and logical. The old way of leadership is based on submitting to people who are more intimidating or older than oneself.

I am certainly not promoting disrespect toward our elders – on the contrary, we love and appreciate them for raising us – but in many cases their advice is not applicable to the dynamics of modern-day society. Unless the older generation commits to adapting to modern-day realities, it is very hard for an educated young person to accept advice or constructive criticism from them. I have learned during my time abroad that experience doesn't always equal maturity, knowledge, good advice or modern-day success formulas. We live in the digital age, where people in their teens and twenties are becoming millionaires on a daily basis, while doing the exact opposite of what their parents and teachers told them to do. These days, not going to college, building a brand, or working from one's computer and phone could be wise decisions, which could lead to financial independence, if done the proper way. Do you now see how it would be difficult for a person who was raised in the 1950s or 60s to effectively lead today's generation, if they don't adapt?

In many ways, SWAL is like an alarm clock: we can either decide to get up or hit the snooze button.

CUT THROUGH COMFORT: TIME IS TICKING

Go to college; get good grades while paying for it with credit; get a job; buy a house with credit (in other words, become a slave to the system); invest in low-risk stocks; pay back credit at monthly intervals for the next forty years; work your tail off for those forty years; and then finally retire, and enjoy five or six years of freedom before you are dead. Does this sound like great advice? Maybe in 1975, but it isn't anymore. Who says that long life is guaranteed? As I write this, the world is dealing with a coronavirus pandemic outbreak, and innocent people are dying every day – some of them probably assumed that they had "time". Do not allow yourself or others to excuse your shortcomings by referencing "time" as your asset.

The old way of leadership is based on paying your dues to the person in charge, and then, maybe ten to fifteen years after they have moved on, you can move into a leadership role. We must let go of this "settling for" mentality, and recognize that our time on this Earth can end in a split second. It is a fact that you can't afford to ignore, so don't wait until you are older or more experienced to make an impact. Regardless of age, all of our clocks are ticking. Just as it is never too early to pursue your dreams, it is also never too late to adapt and thrive in modern times. Start the process now, and don't let your perception of lack or abundance of time become your excuse to settle or wait, while precious moments pass you by.

This is what my coach meant by not falling into the "trap". The trap is the assumption that we have time on our side; so many people delay their plans for the present, and focus all their attention on the future. This is often a healthy practice, but it can also be a trap. Take responsibility for your life now; do not wait until it is too late.

My hope is that the SWAL concept will help you understand that, if you adapt you can make an impact, regardless of where you are in life. Don't wait for the proper education or the perfect time. Don't assume that you are too young to begin, or too old to change. If you truly desire to, you have the ability to not only succeed in your career but, more importantly, impact the lives of others through your leadership. I hope the rest of this book inspires you to take that step and live your legacy.

With that said, let's dive into the nitty-gritty of the Swiss Army Leadership concept.

GRAB THE HANDLE: PERSONAL FOUNDATION

This is, without a doubt, the most essential characteristic of any effective leader. One's mentality is who they are. Some of us are tall and muscular, while others are short and stocky, but our physical presence is mere packaging; the core of who we are as human beings lies between our ears. Our personal foundation defines us.

It is truly fascinating how society has placed such a high premium on physical appearance, while character often takes a back seat – I will be the first to admit that I'm guilty of this. I know that studies have shown that when we physically train our bodies, our minds benefit as well, and I am not disputing this; what I do have a problem with is the motive behind the fitness craze which is prevalent today: we aren't training for our own personal benefit, but rather for the approval of others (e.g. fishing for compliments and *Instagram* likes).

This obsession for attention is causing many people to disregard their own personal development and self-leadership. I know because I experienced it. I remember spending hours in the gym, pumping my muscles, only so that I could impress women and perform better on the football field. I was so consumed with what my muscle training gave to me (girls and football success), that I convinced myself I actually loved training. After that phase of my life ended, I became unmotivated to go to the gym, and realized that I didn't really love working out; I just loved what it gave me.

In order to succeed as a SWALeader, you must grasp the importance of effectively leading yourself, before you can effectively lead others – this means having healthy goals and prioritizing your overall wellbeing.

A strong personal foundation leads to self-confidence and peace of mind.

It is generally assumed that people in powerful positions possess a stable mind and strong personal foundation, but sadly this is not always the case. In fact, these people are often the ones who are suffering the most inside.

From my experience, three things are required to build a strong personal foundation; I call them the *"3 Rs of living"*:

The first one is *REASON*.

Regardless of our title and our responsibilities, we have to believe that our objectives are for a greater cause, whether that be growing a brand which will help others; learning a new strategy or tactic which will make us more valuable; spiritual growth; and/or solving a nagging problem. The key is that this reasoning must go beyond personal or financial benefit; if you're only in it for the money, you are destined for eventual failure. This in no way suggests that money is not important – it definitely is; money is essential for accomplishing goals and pursuing dreams – but the key is not to allow money to become your number one motivation. There is a difference between understanding the importance of money and lusting for it, and as SWALeaders we have to constantly examine ourselves, to make sure we understand this.

I feel that the best way to do this is to develop the mindset of *value*. If we provide value to others in terms of quality leadership, then we will be rewarded for that value.

The second R is *RELATIONSHIPS*.

Human beings were created for interaction. Yes, we all enjoy our moments alone, from time to time, but the quality of our relationships with others will go a long way in developing our own foundation.

I believe there are five types of relationships we must cultivate: *intimate, family, friendships, business* and *spiritual*.

Our intimate relationships will determine whether we build a strong or weak personal foundation. For example, a single man at the grocery store sees a woman he is attracted to, so he strikes up a conversation with her and, lucky for him, he leaves with her phone number! Any guy will tell you that moments like that feel great; they help build self-confidence, which can positively affect other aspects of life. Conversely, the C.E.O. of a big company, who has been married for ten years, is going through an ugly divorce. This is not something he can just shrug off; he has to deal with all the negative emotions, while trying to effectively run a company. This can lead to angry outbursts or health problems. Ed Mylett, a popular influencer and author, said: "We do not just feel emotions; we *do* emotions."

Next, we have family relationships. Despite inevitable disagreements and tension from time to time, nothing can replace the support from one's family members. Our immediate family are the only people who will love us unconditionally, and have our backs all the time. While it is an unfortunate truth that not everyone has the luxury of quality family relationships, it is possible to rise above that disappointment and move forward. Such people attract a great deal of respect and admiration.

An adage says: *"Intimate relationships come and go, but friends last forever."* This is debatable, because it depends on the quality of friends you have. Still, your friendships play a huge role in the development of your personal foundation, and will impact the type of person you become. In simpler terms, we become who we decide to associate ourselves with. If we associate with people who are content working a nine-to-five job in a department store, then there is a good chance we will become content with this as well; if we associate with people who dream big and pursue those dreams, chances are we will do the same. This is why it is so important to have the kind of friendships that will help you grow as a person, and help you build your foundation. Of course, this doesn't mean that all your friends must be wealthy, but I do believe that we need to look for admirable characteristics in others, which can help us grow.

Business relationships are very important, and I like to call them "networking relationships", because that is essentially what business is. We must learn to leverage our business relationships, to create opportunities which help us achieve our goals. The primary purpose of business relationships is value, and this must be mutual; it is not inherently selfish to recognize this fact.

Last but certainly not least are spiritual relationships.

I consider my relationship with God to be my primary spiritual relationship. Without getting into the touchy subject of religion, a spiritual relationship is essentially a belief in a higher power, and relying on that higher power for guidance throughout one's life. Personally, prayer is how my spiritual relationship with God is sustained; I believe that, through prayer, I can receive God's guidance to lead me on the path I'm meant to follow.

The key to a spiritual relationship is faith, and when one is serious about faith, he or she is driven by that faith. Faith grounds one's life in hope and purpose

The final R is *RIGHTEOUSNESS.*

Righteousness is defined as divine or moral law, free from guilt or sin.

Freedom from guilt or sin is an idea which is often disregarded in society and business. While money is obviously a necessity, the love of acquiring it has corrupted a large portion of our society. Unfortunately, there are individuals and organizations so consumed with the amount of money going into their pockets that they lose all sense of morality about how the money is actually acquired. This means that priorities are misplaced and ethics often ignored.

This lack of integrity and corruption is nothing new to mankind; we only need to look at the horrific acts of Adolf Hitler during World War Two, or a more recent example in the Wells Fargo account fraud scandal of 2016: to make a long story short, employees were under pressure to hit quotas and, as a result, were encouraged to order credit cards for "pre-approved" customers without the customers' consent, all the while using their own contact information to prevent customers from discovering the fraud. When it was finally discovered, branch workers and managers were indicted and the managers initially blamed their employees; it wasn't until later in the process that the high-level managers were forced to take responsibility. This is a classic case of the love of money becoming a source of corruption in leadership.

As SWALeaders, we have to make sure that all our actions are done in a righteous manner, which will allow us to be at peace with whatever results may come. Turning a blind eye to corruption and immorality, in favor of personal gain, is one of the most unrighteous acts anyone can commit, yet such acts have become as common as owning a smartphone. Any person with a strong moral compass understands that treating people ethically, and doing one's part to impact others positively, will yield peace of mind and a sense of gratification. As a SWALeader, your decisions must give you peace of mind.

Another aspect of righteousness is doing right by your followers, no matter what. This means prioritizing ethics over personal and financial benefit. We must realize that our success is largely defined by the success of the people in our group; they are a reflection of our own ability to lead effectively, which is a huge responsibility. When righteousness is the motive for all our actions, we sleep well at night and are at peace with results.

In summary, your personal foundation is what holds your success. Just as the handle of a Swiss Army knife holds all its tools inside, the "3Rs" hold our tools within our personal foundation.

TOOL 1: TELLING

More often than not, we associate loud voices with intimidation. But the fact that a person has a loud voice doesn't necessarily mean that he is criticizing you; it is important to hear the context of his message. On the other hand, if someone gives positive reinforcement, they are perceived as inspirational and a joy to be around.

The key here is balance; effective leaders must be good at communicating the intent of their actions. While I agree that actions speak louder than words, we must remember that words are the vehicle for communication. Effective communication is an essential tool for effective leadership development, and I like to use the 70:30 ratio to drive this point home: communication is 70% instruction (usually verbal) and 30% motivation (verbal and action).

Motivational communication is tailored toward bringing out the best in your followers, through the skill of public speaking, as well as personal work ethic and commitment. There is a common misconception that being a motivational speaker means that one must be able to get rousing and emotional responses from their audience, but this isn't reality; a true motivational speaker has the ability to reach people on a personal level, and earn their respect via proper word choice, content and tone – in addition to these words there is consistent action, and the end result is respect. When your team respects you, it is very easy for them to stay motivated, even through the most difficult tasks.

On the other hand, I am fairly certain that we have all been in situations where the leader criticizes and puts the team down, thinking that this will boost performance and make team members respect them. I believe that it's safe to say this approach usually has the opposite effect.

This is regularly seen in the sports arena; it is common to see footage of a coach or team captain before the team, ahead of a game, yelling in an effort to inspire the team. This may get some players initially fired-up and motivated, based on human emotion, but this burst of adrenaline will fizzle out fast when one is faced with the reality of the high stakes involved – at that point, all the yelling and screaming in the world will have no effect on that individual or group performance.

As a former professional quarterback, who has played in seven countries, I've had the opportunity to be around a lot of great coaches and players. I remember a game in Germany, back in 2013, where we were winning by at least twenty points at halftime, and our team spirit and confidence was very high. In Europe, football teams don't usually go into locker rooms during halftime, but rather gather on a shaded patch of grass, to discuss strategy and make necessary adjustments for the second half – this is the reason I could hear the coach from the opposite team yelling and cussing out his players; he told them that they weren't good enough, they sucked at football and that they had better improve their game, or else he would unleash the wrath of a 68-year-old man on them. Now, this man had been a very successful coach in the U.S.A., and had won multiple championships at the high school level – however, all that experience and success were of no use to the German team he was coaching that day; the funny thing was that practically no one could understand him, amidst all that cursing in his deep Southern accent. Although this strategy may have worked in the U.S. at one point, that didn't mean that it would work in Germany. Yes, this guy had been a successful coach in the past, but his present environment and culture was extremely different, and he failed to adjust his coaching and leadership styles accordingly. What his players needed at that moment was instruction and encouragement, to motivate them to do better – not yelling, which only confused and discouraged them further. Not surprisingly, we scored another thirty points in the second half, and beat them about 50-0.

Moral of the story? Effective leaders must learn to adapt to their environment and use both instruction and motivation to get their team(s) to success.

Now, there may be cases when the people you are leading need what I like to call "a kick in the behind". An example of this is when very talented and experienced individuals are underachieving, and fail to realize how their lack of effort undermines the team. People who have accomplished great things in the past could be vulnerable to this mentality, because it is easy to get complacent when you feel you have already arrived at your destination, and "rest on your laurels". A good leader knows how to wake people up without putting them down.

TOOL 2: SHOWING

Effective leadership is about action more than anything else. We can't tell others to do as we say and not as we do. This may seem like an obvious concept, but it is amazing how many self-styled leaders fool people by being all talk and zero corresponding action. I can think of no better example in support of this point than politicians (a majority of them at least). During a presidential election, each candidate resorts to making countless promises and plans of action, in order to get more votes; once elected to office, they take little to no action on the promises they made with such fervor – instead, they blame their opponents for every failure or procrastinate until their time in office is over. While this isn't always the case, it seems to be the norm. Leaders who talk more than act, while making unrealistic promises, aren't to be trusted. Still, it is ironic how we as a society put our trust in these types of individuals to run our world.

In 2017, I received an inquiry about the possibility of playing quarterback in Salzburg, Austria. The coach told me that I could come visit, to get a feel of the city and team, meet some of the players and watch practice. Since it wasn't a tryout, I decided to go dressed like a true Italian: I wore ripped skinny jeans, a deep-cut, slim-fit, V-neck T-shirt, some knock off Ray-Ban sunglasses and light-brown Timberland boots. I felt like a modern-day Joe Namath. After a tour of the city, the coach took me to practice, and I remember the funny looks I was getting from all the players; it was as though they were saying: "This short, pretty boy is a football player? He looks like he should be in a fashion show, not on a football field." I chuckled, because I could tell they were worried and just a bit confused. The offensive coordinator came up to me and asked if I could throw a few balls to the guys. Honestly, I was a bit annoyed because I had been told that this wasn't a tryout, but I decided to humor them and threw a few soft warmup tosses. I then stepped in during team drills, in my stylish street clothes, while everyone else was wearing helmets and shoulder pads – I wish someone had taken a picture, because it was the most ridiculous sight! I wanted to prove a point, so I took the snap and heaved a 60-yard "Hail Mary" pass. No one caught the ball, but my point was made; I just winked at the guys in the huddle and said: "Good enough for you guys?" I was signed after that practice. Moral of the story: I was aware of my capabilities and comfortable with my ability; however, those guys had already dismissed me as the short, pretty boy wearing skinny jeans. It would have made no difference if I just told them that I was a capable quarterback; I needed to show them.

The bottom line: whether in sports, business or daily life, people may at times be convinced by words alone, but in the end they believe what they see.

TOOL 3: CALLING CARD

What is a calling card, and how is this important to the concept of SWAL and effective leadership? It is an idiom which means having special skill(s) or talent(s), which sets an individual apart from others. Effective leaders and successful people usually have at least one trait or skill, which separates, elevates and gives them credibility.

The bottom line is that people want to be led by those who have experience or skill in areas they themselves don't. Society has all too often been scammed by people with fake credentials, and this has resulted in increased skepticism. This skepticism oftentimes makes it difficult for inexperienced people with great potential to be awarded an initial opportunity to prove their worth. As frustrating as the solution may be, often the only way to handle these types of situations is to continue to stay the course and develop these calling card(s), while remaining ready when opportunity knocks. It is important not to get discouraged by rejection, because the world is changing rapidly; it is only a matter of time until your expertise will be in demand and your potential will be realized.

I consider my calling cards to be intercultural competence, strong social skills and public speaking ability. I can easily prove these skills, so they market my credibility as a person who can lead effectively; I can show people photos, tell stories of my time abroad, accept public speaking invitations, or even publish various interviews I have done. To cite one experience, I remember a time when I was living in France. I had a press conference at a local restaurant, about the outlook of the upcoming football season – however, as a 21-year-old kid from rural Pennsylvania, of course I didn't speak any French. For those who aren't aware, France is a very proud country, and speaking English is often looked on in a somewhat negative light. That being said, due to my lack of fluency in French, I was forced to rely on my ability to speak the way in which I already knew. Throughout the interview, I was able to get my point across to the audience by using the tone and pace of my voice, along with confident body language. Sure, I did get some looks of confusion and bewilderment; however, the way in which I spoke allowed me to convince the others that I was a capable person for the job. In this case, the words I was saying were rather insignificant; my confident body language and tone of voice said it all. In this situation, I was faced with the issue of not being able to effectively communicate, due to a language barrier; nevertheless, I relied on my public speaking calling card in order to successfully navigate the interview and prove my credibility to the audience.

In summary, effective leaders need to identify, enhance and utilize their calling card(s), in order to gain and maintain credibility. What if you don't have the real-world experience yet? The solution is simple: educate yourself in relation to where the world is headed. The more you develop yourself, the more the opportunities will emerge for you to gain experience as society advances.

Peter Drucker was a respected pioneer in effective management and leadership in modern society. Before Drucker passed away in 2005, he declared that increasing the productivity of knowledgeable workers was "the most important contribution management needs to make in the 21st century." It is now 2020, and it is clear that his statement was spot on; as technology continues to advance, it is crucial that businesses stay up to date.

Take advertising, for example. The old method included strategies such as renting a billboard or posting an ad, in a newspaper or magazine. These were very expensive methods, even though the target audience was limited. Today, we have options which have a much wider reach and are less expensive: e.g. social media, email and internet advertising. However, not everyone knows how social media platforms work, or they are unwilling to acknowledge the importance of such media – this attitude puts their businesses at a distinct disadvantage.

It is important to emphasize that SWAL doesn't take potential for granted. Just because someone doesn't have experience doesn't mean that they aren't capable of great leadership. In fact, in today's ever-changing world, experience may be more of a hindrance than an advantage. Develop skillsets which are relevant in these modern times, but remember to stay focused, because "a jack of all trades is a master of none". This is the principle of specificity.

TOOL 4: CARING

The knowledge that you are cared for is an assuring and heartwarming feeling. Just as parents care for their children, or siblings care for each other, SWALeaders genuinely care for their followers and have their best interests at heart.

However, this is easier said than done, for obvious reasons; caring for someone requires that you have some form of relationship with them. Mothers start to develop a relationship with their child before the baby is even born. According to *Health Direct*, at 26 weeks gestation an unborn baby may react to noises both inside and outside the mother's body, and may be soothed by the sound of her voice. This explains why the bond between a mother and child is often unbreakable. Life outside the womb is very different, however.

The world of business and sports are very cutthroat. Players are released from the team when their bodies fail them, and people often lose their jobs without warning or a justifiable reason. This makes it very difficult to truly develop relationships and care for the ones you are guiding. So, how do effective leaders genuinely care for someone with whom they may have to part ways? One word: honesty.

In business and sports, honesty goes a long way. Players and employees in the United States and most European countries do not want things to be sugar-coated. As a leader, it is your job to give subordinates the facts first, and then make each one aware of his specific role in the team or group.

Also, take the time to have one-on-one chats with each person in the group – this is also critical in learning about the individuals and getting a feel for their personalities, and how they may respond to certain methods of instruction. Taking time out to talk about aspects of their personal life, such as their mental health, families and friends, and suggesting ways they can improve themselves, is a personal touch which goes a long way in earning respect and showing how much you truly care. I've discovered that it is important to ask your followers what goals they have set for themselves, within and outside the organization. If you are willing to help someone achieve his or her personal goals, even if it has little or no benefit to you, it shows you truly care about the individual.

One of the big dilemmas that many companies face today is the coming and going of employees. A lot of businesses struggle with the idea of committing time and money to training their employees, due to the fact that they may be training them to help rival companies. The bottom line is – like it or not – many people are always looking for greener pastures. They may be with your organization one day, then suddenly a new, more lucrative offer comes along and, just like that, they are gone, taking all of the training you invested in to their new job with one of your competitors. While this is certainly an unfortunate reality, it is our responsibility as effective leaders to care for and provide the best for our employees, as long as they are in the same building as us. We must also remember that by prioritizing our followers/employees, we are not only doing right by them as individuals, we are also setting up our business for the best opportunity to succeed. A quote by Mr. Henry Ford justifies this ideology; Ford famously said: "The only thing worse than training your employees and having them leave is not training them and having them stay." Don't let negligence turn into disaster. The best thing we can do in these types of situation is to treat and care for people so well that they do not want to leave.

Another roadblock in regard to the act of caring is that most leadership positions often overlap with business. People often believe that they should keep their distance because, eventually, they will have to let an employee go or fire a member of their following. That kind of leadership doesn't make any positive impact on others. Leaders will undoubtedly have to make tough decisions, which may negatively affect people's lives, but effective leaders must find a way to show they care while being honest, and not burning any bridges.

In my freshman year of college, I was unhappy with my status on the football team; I was a backup, and had no real chance of becoming a starter anytime soon. I had a meeting with my coach at the end of the season and he was very honest with me, and told me that with the starting quarterback from the previous season returning, it was unlikely I would get on the field during the next season in that position. He then suggested I move to the defensive side of the ball, and try to play safety. I was angry at first, and understandably so, but deep down I also respected his honesty. He then asked what my goals were as a player, which surprised me, because I didn't think he cared that much (considering the fact that I wasn't a contributing player on the field at that time). I told him that I wanted to have a chance to compete for the starting quarterback position in the next season. What he then said surprised me even further: "I know a few coaches at other schools who have spots open for next season. If you'd like, I can give them a call and put in a good word for you." He said that he would hate to lose me, but if my goals were to be a starter in the next season, I had better chances elsewhere.

This made me respect him even more. His honesty and willingness to take the time to help me achieve my personal goal (despite the absence of any personal gain) stuck with me. This is what a caring leader does. Human beings have emotions, and effective leaders recognize this. They also find a way to earn respect, notwithstanding any negative vibe.

EXTRA TOOL: CARING IS REMEMBERING – THE POWER IN A NAME

One of the best ways to show that you care is by simply using someone's name when talking with them, but this is quite difficult for a lot of folks. Why? According to *psychologytoday.com*, some of the reasons we forget people's names is the fact that they are arbitrary, don't have synonyms or references, often contain multiple words and are often low-frequency terms. Effective leaders cannot use these excuses not to remember the names of people, because it can potentially rub people the wrong way. The power of remembering and using people's names in conversation goes a long way toward gaining their respect.

This may not seem like a big deal, in a world where it is acceptable to say something like: "I'm so sorry, I'm just terrible with names; could you tell me your name again?" While this is by no means impolite, we need to be more intentional about not putting ourselves in that situation. As leaders who aspire to be successful, it is vital that we remember and use the names of the people we are leading. This simple gesture will have a huge impact on how we are perceived. Some might say: "I have so much to do; I don't have the time to remember everyone's name." This may be true, but you have to decide what type of leader you want to be. When there is a will, there is a way. In the words of Hall of Fame quarterback Steve Young: "If you want to earn respect, know the names of everyone in the building." I remember hearing those words while watching a football documentary, and they have stuck with me, and proven very helpful in my leadership experiences.

In his famous book *How to Win Friends and Influence People*, author Dale Carnegie says: *"A person's name is, to that person, the sweetest, most important sound in any language."* I can personally attest to this. I was a 20-year-old man playing football in a rural Polish suburb, on a team full of older men in their late twenties, thirties and even forties, with little to no knowledge of the English language. Regardless, I was immediately thrust into a leadership role and was expected to guide them to victory. This is where I truly realized the power of one's name. Although I spoke no Polish, I took the time to (as Carnegie said) remember the sweetest and most important sound of each individual. I printed out the team roster with the profile pictures of each player, and studied the faces and the names of each player on the team, until I knew them all by heart. This proved very crucial to our team's success, because the players respected the fact that I cared enough to learn and use their names when I addressed them. I definitely butchered some of the pronunciations, but it was clear that they appreciated the effort. Eventually, I was able to learn some of the important Polish words, in order to have a basic conversation, but by learning the teammates' names, I had laid a solid foundation which would aid me during that season.

TOOL 5: RELATING

No human being likes the feeling of being alone 100% of the time; we all want to be able to safely talk to someone about our experiences, at one point or another. The ability to give proper guidance is an important attribute of an effective leader. The power of relating to people has amazing potential.

If we can empathize with people and help them gain new perspectives about their situations, leadership takes on a new and deeper meaning. We all have demons we have to deal with, and when you let your followers know they are not alone in their fight, you give them hope that things will get better. This is a skill which is invaluable in life and business.

Finally, a story which is not football related! I was waiting in line at a train ticket kiosk in Vienna, to purchase a ticket to Salzburg, and an older couple was in front of me. When it became their turn to use the touch screen self-service system, they had a bit of difficulty. I could hear the people behind me starting to complain about how long they were taking, and some even had the audacity to yell: "Come on, other people have trains to catch!" This is when I decided to help them, but it was difficult at first, because they didn't speak any English or German. The people behind me got angrier the longer it took to figure things out, and a younger man even tried to cut in front of them, but I firmly told him that I was going to help them, until they got their ticket. I understood their situation and could empathize, because I knew what it was like to be in a foreign country where few people speak your language: it is stressful, and it certainly doesn't help when you are being yelled at by strangers.

I had to think fast, because things were escalating quickly, so I pointed to the departure board above the kiosk and asked: "Where?" The gentleman looked up at the board and signaled the number two, which was a 12:30 p.m. departure to Prague. I keyed in the information needed for two adult tickets, and signaled for him to confirm the information before the purchase. Problem solved. I even let the annoyed guy behind me buy his ticket before me. After I purchased my ticket and headed to my terminal, I heard: "Hey!" When I turned, it was the gentleman, who had written a *"thank you"* note on *Google Translate*. The note also mentioned that I was welcome to visit him and his wife in Dubai anytime, and he gave me his business card. I was surprised, and caught a bit off-guard, but I smiled and gestured my thanks. On the train ride from Vienna to Salzburg, I was able to translate the Arabic, with the miracle of technology, and it turned out he was a very prominent lawyer in Dubai.

I haven't had the time to take him up on his offer, but we have remained in touch, and I am confident that one day we will meet again and something great will come from it.

I am certainly glad that I chose to "relate" that day in Vienna, and I learned two things from this experience: the first is the power of making valuable connections and building long-term relationships; the second lesson I learned is that looks or situations can be deceiving. The language barrier in Vienna, Austria disguised an accomplished lawyer in Dubai.

Look for opportunities to use your past adversity to relate and assist others through their present adversity.

TOOL 6: OBSERVING

Life is not a lottery. People who make decisions without insight or knowledge are usually destined for failure. This may be as simple as buying a "bargain-priced" item, without reading the reviews or checking the seller's background, and in the end the product turns out to be junk. Or, it could be as serious as investing a large sum of money in a stock, based only on word of mouth, without doing proper research.

This rule applies to SWAL. We, as aspiring leaders, must learn to make more decisions based on observations and analysis. It is your job as an effective leader to become a master at observing your followers' individual needs, strengths and weaknesses. Treat others not the way you want to be treated, but how *they* want to be treated.

As a person in a leadership role, you will come across people of all different cultures, religions, financial/social statuses, political beliefs, age, race, gender, physical ability and mental states. It is your job to recognize the building block characteristics of each individual – and, trust me, it is not that difficult and does not take too much time to grasp; it is more of a natural feel for the situation than anything. You can easily practice and develop this skill by interacting.

For example, now, as an American football coach for teenagers, I am getting a lot of experience during our 3-day-per-week practices. It took me a while, but I began to recollect just how sensitive and crucial a time one's teenage years are, in the grand scheme of their personal development; their bodies, mentality, beliefs, priorities and overall view of life are changing and developing drastically. I have a few players, on my various teams in Italy and Austria, whom I have observed and realized just how delicate their state of minds are – even more so than most teenagers. I realized this because I was also one of those over-sensitive young men growing up. Some teens are just more delicate than others. But I would also put a positive spin on that, and say that some teens are more aware of what human emotion is than others. It is interesting to look at these young men and see each of their reactions to various forces around them. For example, some adolescents are more open and humored by jokes against them, despite the teasing coming from a peer.

This is where it becomes important, as effective leaders, to dig deeper into our own understanding of specific people. Oftentimes, when we observe one's reactions, we can get a lot of inside information about how their lives are operating outside of the time we spend with them. This goes back to the previous tool of caring. Caring is relevant here, because observing is a major aspect of caring; when we take the time to observe an individual's reactions, we can then take that information and apply it to our strategy for leading them.

For example, there was one young man I was coaching, who would flinch every time I raised my hand to greet him; I couldn't have felt worse about the situation. After talking with a few other coaches and thinking more about it, I realized that he likely interpreted my signal for a high-five as a fist preparing for a punch. Naturally, this caused me to assume that he was being bullied or abused in one way or another. At first, I wasn't sure exactly what to do; I didn't know if I should bring it up with his parents (which I probably should have) or if I should have a private talk with him, so I called him over after practice one day, to talk privately. Understanding that this young man was very sensitive, I did not want to ask him directly if he was being bullied by anyone at home, school or (God forbid) one of the other players on the team; I decided to take a more present-moment approach, and simply asked him: "Hey buddy, how was your day? You look a bit down in the dumps." As expected, he didn't really give me a straight answer; as a typical teenager, he said: "I'm okay, Coach; just a bit tired from school." Of course he would say that; that is exactly the answer I would have given twelve years ago, as well. I knew, at that moment, that the best thing I could do for him was to be a shining light in his day. It hurt me to admit it, but I couldn't control what was happening to him when he was not at football practice; however, during the time when he was, I knew I had to make that the best experience of his day, by encouraging him. I had hopes that my compassionate behavior toward him would provide enough joy to keep him pushing through the rough times, knowing that at football practice he would receive encouragement and joy. I also decided to give him a handshake rather than a high-five from that point on – that seemed to help his flinching, as well. It truly pained me to see this kid going through this kind of adversity, but I hoped that maybe my encouragement would be something that he could look forward to.

I also made it a point of emphasis to coach him based on his effort, rather than his on-field performance. Regardless of talent level, when someone gives you their 100% effort, that is really all anyone can ask for. The difference is that effort combined with talent usually translates into production.

Conversely, the same effort with a lack of talent doesn't necessarily lead to production – but, then again, this statement depends on how one defines "production". Most people define production as something like physical output or level of performance; SWALeaders define production as mental output and performance.

Let me explain using the same example: if this young man had been able to improve his motivation and develop a positive mental attitude from my mentorship, then that is production.

It is so common nowadays to see coaches and bosses fail at their overall job, because they preach treating every player the same, and therefore hold the same performance expectations for everyone (physical and mental). This may work at the elite levels of the sporting world, or in huge corporations, but this is highly likely to be a recipe for disaster when dealing with mentally and physically vulnerable teenagers, or people with disgruntled pasts and mental states.

As briefly noted, this flaw in leadership also proves true for many adults. There are many grown people who are insecure about themselves, and break down when it comes to receiving pressure or criticism. On the other hand, others may thrive in these situations.

I believe that the reason most coaches and people in power refuse to change their ways is because they are often guilty of only accounting for the people who produce physical results for them, and contribute to their personal job security. All humans are selfish by nature. Why? Because their jobs are based on the physical results. Most of their talented players or employees (producers) know how to respond to being challenged and pushed. However, when self-proclaimed leaders solely focus on the people who produce for them, they are doing much more internal and external damage than they realize; it begs the question: do they actually care about the others, who may not be contributing to the physical results? Sadly, more often than not, the answer is likely no – which is an unfortunate reality, because who's to say that these individuals, currently going through tough times, or perhaps lacking necessary physical and mental capabilities, can't eventually develop under your mentorship, and eventually become major contributors?

Mentorship is an amazing and fulfilling opportunity to inspire and truly make an impact on someone's life. These are the moments which truly bring one joy. Nevertheless, a vast number of coaches/bosses miss the big picture, because of their lust for expedited results in the short term. This isn't always their fault, as much as it is a response to the demand society makes for immediate production. This is where SWAL seeks to make a change in this mindset.

The truth of the matter is that society's lust for reckless production is causing a lot of potential to go unnoticed. It is also manipulating natural human emotion, by disregarding others who aren't currently performing up to standard. This mentality turns bosses into robots, as they scan the data and make decisions strictly based on production. The idea of personal connection is becoming an extinct trait, in a lot of cases. I can rightly say, from experience, that contributing to another human's growth and development, while playing a role in their rise from life's depths, is undoubtedly a more rewarding feeling than any amount of money one can earn, or number of wins between the lines or in business. When, while acting in a leadership role, you are able to influence and inspire people to change and turn their life around, that is when you have achieved what I like to call "Leadership Utopia". When you arrive at this point, where you are willingly able to sacrifice financial and personal reward for the ability to change lives, you have become a true, effective leader.

The irony here is that these moments will also shape you, just as much (if not more) than the people you have impacted. I will never forget when I learned this lesson; it was January of 2017. At that time, I had been coaching a group of 14 to 19-year-old kids for the past two years, while living in Naples, Italy. I had the opportunity to see and witness the growth of these young men, over this two-year span. I can truly say that I developed a special relationship with those players, and I began to perceive them as the little brothers I'd never had. However, there was one player in particular who sticks out in my mind, when I reflect on my time in Naples: a player of mine who, admittedly, wasn't the most talented, by any means. His name was Marco. Despite his (at the time) lacking physical ability, the one thing that Marco did possess was a desire and passion to improve. He would constantly come to practice early, and ask me to work with him on his catching ability, and his learning of the team's playbook, so that he could earn the chance to play more. I was amazed by his determination and maturity for his age. At fourteen years old, while the other players would be jokingly throwing the ball back and forth, or haphazardly tackling each other to the ground before practice, he was either off to the side doing catching drills, or sitting in the locker room, studying his playbook.

Unfortunately for him, he suffered an injury to his right shoulder in practice, and ended up needing surgery, which sidelined him for most of the two seasons I was there coaching. Still, the most impressive thing about Marco was his positive attitude and commitment. Despite not being able to play, while having to learn to write with his other hand in a crucial school year, he kept coming to practice, simply because he loved being there.

He became my right-hand man, as far as helping me prepare for practices and coaching the others, as well – after all, he had a better grasp of the playbook than anyone on the team. So, here was a 14-year-old kid, who would rather come to watch and learn football than be with his family or friends, or worry about his important exams.

There came a time when I had to leave Naples for another job offer, and he approached me after a meeting in a restaurant, where I said an emotional goodbye to my players. I will never forget his words: "Coach Zach... I just wanted to say that you are the reason I love the game of football. You are a great coach and a great role model. Thank you for standing by me and helping me, and for giving me hope in my toughest time. I will never forget you."

Now, there was nothing in my job description that said I had to inspire players and help change their lives; my job was to prepare the kids to play football, and help them become winners on the field. This is when I learned how truly little weight a job description carries, in the grand scheme of our true purpose. All I know is that, to this day, when I begin to question myself and my purpose in life, I think back to the words of young Marco, and they inspire me to keep going.

Moral of the story: take the time to observe and understand who people really are, what drives them, what they go through and how you can be their shining light, in their time of darkness.

TOOL 7: CHALLENGING

Those of us who have been in the fight long enough have ample experience to know that life is a challenge. So, if life is a challenge, why should we expect anything to be easy? Despite this constant cliché, far too many of us in today's society are looking for a quick, easy fix in regard to our problems.

I must say this fact is not always related to our own fault or realization; the outlandish expectations which many hold can be rooted in the morals by which modern society abides: we are constantly bombarded with phony ads, subscriptions, masterclasses, *YouTube* videos about how to make $10,000 a day, and how to become physically fit by wearing a vibrating belt. We have all heard the saying: *"If it is easy, it probably isn't worth having."* That being said, so many of us disregard this ideology, when we see people who we have never even heard of falsely claim that this so-called "easy-way" actually exists and works. Why is this?

Because we as human beings are suckers for glamour. Glamorous bodies, cars, mansions, women, men and the cash. If someone films themselves standing in front of a mansion in California, with a Lamborghini in the driveway, we become addicted to anything that comes out of his mouth. The reality is that all glamour will eventually lead to sadness, unless it is matched by impact.

The process of becoming an effective leader isn't glamorous. There are no three-day six-pack belts, or $10,000 per day internet hacks.

When you live the SWAL lifestyle you can't be seduced or fueled strictly by monetary means. SWALeaders are driven to build and develop ourselves from within (our personal foundation), via impact on others. When we can impact, the financial success will come naturally.

I recently read a book called *The Millionaire Fastlane* by J.D. Demarco – don't let the title fool you. At one point in the book, he says: *"Impact millions, and you become worth millions."* I am not saying that we should seek to impact strictly for the motive of making millions; I am saying that when we shift our focus and our aspirations to helping others, rather than chasing money, the rest will take care of itself. And, when it doesn't, at least we can be at peace knowing our actions resulted in true, meaningful impact. When we build our personal foundation around this belief, we naturally put ourselves in the best position to earn our personal/financial success, all while truly experiencing wholesome fulfilment.

When we take easy glamour out of the picture, we can now re-apply this ideology: *"If it is easy, it probably isn't worth having."* That being said, there is no such thing as easy leadership, and becoming an effective leader is definitely worth it. Just like a "magic muscle belt", if it is easy as a leader, it's not real leadership. This statement has two meanings: the first and obvious being simply the fact that being an effective leader is not easy. It will be one of the most challenging tasks we take on in our lives, if we are pursuing leadership the right way. The challenges we face are not only specific to ourselves, but also to the people we are mentoring. These challenges have the potential to overwhelm those who are expecting an easy ride to the top, with all the credit and accolades being thrown their way.

The second aspect of this is the idea that we, as aspiring SWALeaders, are responsible for challenging our followers in a way that they have the opportunity to develop into the best versions of themselves under our tutelage. An effective leader has the ability to challenge their pupils in a way which will inspire them to become great; inspiring and challenging are almost interchangeable in this sense. In my view, inspiration is a product of being challenged.

For example, there is a general rule that, if you want to become a more productive and inspired individual, you should form your network around a group of people who are more successful than you. Thus, by interacting with them, your old way of operating will naturally be challenged, and in turn you will develop a sense of inspiration to reach new heights. This can be a very useful strategy to adopt.

On the other hand, it is not to be forgotten that the first step in growth is being able to challenge ourselves from within. Before we even think about surrounding ourselves with quality people, we first have to realize the flaws of our current mindset and lifestyle – from that point, we can challenge ourselves to seek change and adjust accordingly. Without realizing the first step, we will simply continue to erode in our old, ineffective ways, being blind to our reality. Most people fail to realize that, in order to accept the challenge that any leadership position is sure to present, we must first challenge ourselves to look within, and commit to a lifestyle that SWALeaders must undertake.

I have grown to realize that those who accept challenges accept reality, because reality is full of challenges. Also, those who expect "easy" accept failure, because easy and failure live under the same roof. This may be somewhat of a playful statement, but I have learned this the hard way. I once thought I had it all figured out, and that I had won the battle with life: I had the job of my dreams, living in a beautiful city, in an apartment near the beach, with plenty of friends; I was also in a leadership position at my job, and didn't have many people to answer to. I had won, right? Wrong. Just when my life seemed to be at an all-time high, I suddenly lost that job and lost that apartment and lost those so-called friends, who no longer wanted to associate with me, now that my status and glamour were taken away.

Looking back at the situation, I realized that I was the one at fault; I fell into the trap of becoming blind to my impending reality, without a real backup plan and/or sustainable income, outside of playing football. I guess I got caught up in the "Neapolitan Way", of simply living for the moment, drinking my espressos and eating my pizza portafoglio (folded pizza). While this can be a very beautiful and amazing way to live, the lack of long-term security can be alarming, when one stops and realizes how quickly it can take a turn for the worse.

I learned this the hard way. Here I was, in southern Italy, with no job, no place to live, no legal documents and no cash flow of any sort. However, to my own admission of insanity, I always thought that, when it was time to move on to my post-athletic career, it would somehow just happen for me. At this point, my ego was big enough that I assumed someone would come calling for my services because of who I was, when in reality I was a nobody. I expected easy, and began to accept failure as a result.

I became depressed, and it seemed as if I was blindly waiting for someone to rescue me from this financially unstable lifestyle I was living. I began to take erratic actions, to try and get myself out of this rut. I randomly applied for jobs on *LinkedIn*, for which I had no qualifications, because I was expecting an easy, quick fix. After all, I was Zach Hoffman, professional European quarterback and fitness guru. I looked good, played well and traveled the world at a young age, so life should be great, right? Someone must want me, right? I was sadly mistaken.

It took me a while to realize that it wasn't society who was at fault; I had purely failed myself. That young, strong, independent, determined guy I used to be slowly became a lazy, depressed and dependent gypsy, living in a country where he didn't even speak the language. At this time, I am confident that I was the only American "gypsy" in the world!

It reached the point where I finally reasoned with myself, enough to pause and really think about the direction my life was going. I realized that I had stopped challenging myself to achieve greatness and to be different. I suddenly became content just being a normal member of society. I no longer strove for new heights; I now was settling for mediocrity.

With this state of mind, I was also in no position to be an effective leader. How could I preach and challenge people to strive for greatness, when I was the one settling and procrastinating? The answer was I couldn't. I had lost my identity, and I had been through hell and back in the process; I lost my money, my job, my apartment(s), a lot of friends and most of my pride.

Most would say something like: "Zach, why didn't you just ask your family for help, or just go back to America?" Well, that is a very viable question. The answer is that I was too stubborn and embarrassed. I didn't want to show my family that I had failed. I wanted to put on a façade that everything was okay and that I was doing fine, in order to give them peace of mind that I was living the life I had always dreamed of. I may have been a shell of myself at this point in my life, but somehow I was able to maintain just enough pride and persistence; I simply was unwilling to make that call to my mother, and tell her that I needed her to send me money for food, or to ask her to book me a flight home, because I had no place to sleep.

Why? Because, despite my blatant flaws, deep down I knew that I made this choice to live in Europe and I had to live with it. In the end, I knew that I had to get myself back on my feet.

So I persevered, finding small (often illegal) jobs, just to make ends meet; coaching football on the side, in order to cover my apartment costs; constantly moving from one place to another, all to bring me where I am today. Now, three years, three countries and fifteen different apartments later, I am still in a battle, like a lot of us are.

However, my mindset has changed. I no longer expect it to be easy. I accept life's challenges. I am now living in reality, rather than the fantasy world of a professional athlete. I know I have a long way to go, but I am thankful for life's challenges. They have given me an awakening and helped me understand the person I must become, in order to have the impact I desire to leave on this world. My biggest fear and inspiration are that I will die, having not made any impact at all in making this tiny, blue and green speck a better place. This prospect haunts me.

As aspiring leaders, we all must become experts on handling challenges, and understanding that they will be our reality. The good news is that reality doesn't have to break us. We have the power to overcome these challenges and put our stamp on this Earth. Accept challenges as a reality and embrace them, as if your life and legacy depend on them. The reality is, they do.

TOOL 8: TIMING

Timing is everything.

We have all heard this phrase at one point or another in our lives, and it applies to multiple aspects of life. Maybe we applied for that dream job and didn't receive it. Then, we were comforted by our own thoughts or the words of our peers and mentors, saying that the timing wasn't right. On the other hand, maybe we were unemployed and struggling to make ends meet when, just before our situation took a turn for the worse, we got that phone call saying we have been hired. Or, on the lighter side, maybe we tell a joke at the wrong time and someone gets offended, or we wake up ten minutes after our alarm goes off and miss the bus.

Timing is truly everything. We use time as a means of structure for our daily plans, and a means to set deadlines to accomplish our goals and tasks.

The importance of timing, in relation to SWAL and effective leadership, is no exception. We, as aspiring leaders, must utilize appropriate timing in nearly everything we do. For example, we must set a timeline for our goals, in order to not get side-tracked. We must know exactly what tasks need to be accomplished, along with the exact timeframe we have to complete them. One may also call this "organization" – and yes, there is absolutely a correlation. We organize our time in order to develop clear goals, with a clear vision of the results we seek.

Timing must also be utilized on a personal level, with others. We must understand the importance of proper timing, in relation to our followers' capabilities, as well as their readiness to be pushed or challenged. This can be tricky to align with the expectations we set.

Sometimes, we enter a leadership role with little to no idea of the skills, knowledge, experience and mentality of the people we are leading. Maybe, after some time, we find out that our original plan of action does not align with the current capabilities or personalities of our followers. Therefore, effective leaders must become masters at adjusting their timing, in order to best accommodate the group's needs. On the flip side, maybe we enter a situation where we have underestimated the abilities and readiness of the group. In this case, we know that we can push them to higher levels, and adjust our goals and timing accordingly.

Getting even more personal, effective leaders also have to know and understand the use of *situational* timing. Situational timing refers to making decisions which will affect the current life situation of one or more of your followers.

For example, looking at the negative side first, imagine you have recently noticed one of your pupils has displayed a sudden change in personality within the past week. After asking him about it, he tells you that he recently lost a close family member and it is taking a toll on his state of mind. In this case, we must realize that this person should not be put in any situations which require a deadline or an increase in stress. We must give him support and time to heal before we re-elevate our expectations for him; it is appropriate to wait until his original personality has returned to its normal state. This may sound like common sense practice; however, as mentioned before, the unbridled passion for production and results can often blind people to these types of situations.

Looking at the positive side, maybe we notice a recent drive and intensity in one of our pupils. It becomes clear that our expectations for them are being well-exceeded. In this case, we as effective leaders must understand this situation, and react by elevating our expectations to accommodate for their increasing capabilities. This will serve to keep them motivated and interested. It is our responsibility as leaders to look after situations such as these, though this takes great observation, and people skills specific to each individual. It is important that we do not let anyone fall behind by becoming overwhelmed or, conversely, being left alone without being challenged to improve, when he is ready to take that next step.

I myself was at one point on the negative side of situational timing. Thankfully, I was under the council of a great leader, who recognized I wasn't myself and offered his support and guidance. As a young college student, I was struggling with an accounting course; after initially being motivated, my efforts weren't producing results. I became frustrated and even, at one point, stopped showing up for the class. But my professor realized my frustration and reached out to me, via email; he offered to start meeting with me for extra tutoring, two times per week, in preparation for the big midterm exam. I appreciated his offer and accepted it. Despite my preparation and his help, I did not pass the midterm. I became even more unmotivated and down on myself after that; I began to wonder if I would ever be able to pass this course and, as an avid pessimist, immediately began running through all the negative outcomes which would follow. Thankfully, my professor saw something in me that I didn't; he pulled me aside and encouraged me to pick myself up and refocus my mind, in order to pass the final exam.

We continued to meet after that, and he continued to try to help me. Despite my lack of motivation within myself, the fact that he saw something in me gave me enough energy to dig deeper. Thanks to the fact that he realized my vulnerable situation, he was able to encourage me to keep going. Due to his ability to reel me back into focus, I ended up passing the final exam, with a grade in the top five percent of the class. Without his leadership, I am sure this wouldn't have been possible.

That is why we, as aspiring leaders, must realize and take action, during the times when our followers need us the most. Timing, especially situational timing, is truly everything, and we must accept this fact and take responsibility, to guide each individual during times of both triumph and angst.

TOOL 9: NURTURING

When most of us hear the word "nurturing", we often tend to think of something relating to an infant or toddler, just as a mother nurtures her child. Nurturing has quite a simplistic yet effectively written definition:

"to develop further"

Just as a mother raises and develops her child, SWALeaders are responsible for the nourishment and development of their followers. No, I don't mean in the same way in which a mother does; thankfully, there are no dirty diapers and breastfeeding going on here! The term "nurturing", in relation to SWAL, takes on the concept of guiding one in the right direction – more specifically, as aspiring leaders, guiding the group toward becoming believers and contributors toward the said goal or purpose. We need to create an atmosphere where all people are buying into something greater than themselves.

Most of the time, a person in a leadership role will face challenges in the practice of nurturing. There will surely be some backlash and resentment toward some of the decisions you make for the betterment of the group, rather than separate individuals. As mentioned previously, people are selfish by nature; along with ourselves, everyone within a team or group naturally and understandably wants to achieve individual success. At least, we hope so, because otherwise they probably aren't motivated or qualified to contribute to the group's goals (leading oneself). Oftentimes, the act of nurturing is carried out by helping to instill a collective mindset of putting others before yourself, and putting the group's success before any type of personal gain.

Nurturing also implies that we, as aspiring leaders, use our experiences and knowledge to help steer people away from the path which will lead to mistakes we have ourselves made. This idea is a lot like parenting: part of the job of good parents is to try and help their child/children avoid various mistakes they have made in their own life. This, in turn, will hopefully help the child to avoid unnecessary adversity, therefore increasing the likelihood of faster maturity and development.

The act of nurturing is also prevalent in athletics. For example, in the world of professional sports there is a constant cycling of players within the various leagues, which occurs year in and year out. The amazing and ironic part of this system is found within the logistics behind this "player-cycling". Basically, there are the veteran players, who have all the experience and past success, yet their skills and talents are deteriorating due to Father Time (old age) and/or injury; it is only a matter of time until their bodies fail them and they are forced into retirement. That being said, there is an unwritten rule which applies to these veteran players: they are expected to accept the responsibility (though a lot of times reluctantly) of nurturing and helping to prepare the new, younger players to carry on the quality and legacy of the game, once their careers come to an end. The ironic part of all this is that these veteran players are essentially grooming these younger players to become their replacements, consequently taking away their jobs. Despite the occasional outliers, the majority of these veteran players understand and adhere to this unwritten rule; it is perceived by most as their duty, as a quality leader and ambassador, to give back to the game which gave them a means of livelihood. Many see it as a great responsibility, to make sure the team will thrive and continue to achieve at a high level, throughout ensuing generations. This is why the top professional sports leagues, such as the N.F.L., N.B.A., M.L.B., N.H.L. and the various European soccer leagues, have continued to thrive over the years; the constant cycle of player movement in and out of the game, all while maintaining high quality and entertaining performance, is largely due to the practice of nurturing.

The same can be said in the corporate world. For example, when the manager of a company hits the age of sixty and starts looking toward retirement, he/she has a responsibility, as an effective leader, to make sure the company will maintain its success long after he/she departs. This means that they ought to take the time to groom (nurture) their replacements.

However, unless it is a family business, this idea is often taken on with reluctance. In a lot of cases, the fact of the matter is that stubbornness can habitually play a role in the act of nurturing. Why? People who have a proven track record of success and leadership often have a rather large ego, and an unwillingness to simply train a person to eventually take their job (or, God forbid, do it better than they did). It is a shame that these issues come up so often. This is, once again, simply the element of human nature taking over. Nevertheless, it is a big reason why quality leadership is often hard to come by.

As a responsible and effective leader, one must train themselves to fight against the egotistical voice within all of us. Whether we want to admit it or not, a large majority of leaders in sports and business have rather large egos; having a large ego is part of what gives them the ability to earn a leadership role in the first place. However, there comes a time when one must put their ego aside and accept the responsibility which others accepted before them. If there is a history of ineffective leadership, then leaders must take it upon themselves to set an example, and start the trend for future generations to follow.

When it all boils down, nurturing is truly our most important job as the next generation of successful leaders; this is the aspect which will surely have the most impact on society, our reputation and our own personal satisfaction. The biggest challenge is accepting that you can't and won't be around forever; one's legacy is all that can live on and be remembered – so make sure you leave yours. Make your legacy and leadership ability one that is remembered and modeled well after you are gone.

I must also clear up a common misconception about legacy. Most people correlate the term "legacy" with fame and fortune. This couldn't be more inaccurate. In fact, Merriam-Webster defines the term "legacy" in two ways, on two different sides of the spectrum. The first definition states:

"a gift by will, especially of money or other personal property"

This is definitely not what legacy means in SWAL terminology. This definition implies that one's legacy is merely physical, meaning it can be taken away or destroyed.

The second definition states:

"something transmitted by or received from an ancestor or predecessor, or from the past"

This is the definition which is correct in terms of SWAL. However, it is important to remember that the "something" listed at the beginning of this definition is not a physical item or monetary item; as SWALeaders, our "something" must be legendary. Being "legendary" means impacting people's lives in such a way that they will use the same impact you made to pay it forward, to future generations. This is often a process which goes unnoticed, unless one is a professional athlete, actor/actress or billionaire, but there are plenty of "hometown legends", whose impact is still felt within their family or community.

It is important not to associate the term "legendary" with fame, because there are plenty of "hometown legends" who have set the standard for others, within various communities around the world.

Legendary status within your community is the goal of a SWALeader. If we have enough effective leaders working in their own designated community, the result will be a new generation of modern-day competence and success. Creating a positive impact, which has a ripple-effect felt by future generations, long after you are gone, should be one's ultimate resolve.

THE REALITY: MISTAKES WILL BE MADE

No matter how old or young you are, you will make mistakes, and people in leadership roles are no exception. What a lot of aspiring leaders fail to understand is the fact that their mistakes will be magnified and critiqued much more than the typical individual. This is where a lot of people who are new to leadership roles run into problems.

The process of realizing, accepting and adapting to the fact that your once-unnoticed mistakes now carry much more weight takes time. The key is that we use these mistakes to further our development, and not let them reoccur. That is why it's important to avoid ignorance in regard to our mistakes; admit them, make amends and move on with a lesson learned for future development.

I will never forget one of the major mistakes I made during my time in Europe. I was a young 22-year-old, who had just finished college, and I was signed to play quarterback for a team in southern Bavaria, Germany, along with another American player from California. At first, things were great; the other players on the team were awesome guys, and the coaches were also fun to play for. That said, being the immature young man that I was, I nit-picked a few things to complain about. Looking back on the situation today, I realize that these issues were not a big deal, yet at that time they caused me to make some foolish decisions.

Let's start with the first issue: housing. I had no problem with the accommodation we were provided. The other player and I lived together in a spacious guest house, with all the necessities to live comfortably. The issue we had was the location: Hanfeld, Germany. Below is a very old picture of this little town and, as I look back, it truly portrays the atmosphere in which I was living. I want to be clear that I'm not dissing

Hanfeld; it just wasn't an ideal living place for a 22-year-old American looking for a European adventure. I remember the other American player and I used to joke with each other that in Hanfeld there were more chickens than people (which isn't an exaggeration).

This led to our second complaint: the lack of transportation; in Hanfeld there was not a huge need for public transportation services. There was a bus which came once or twice every two or three hours, but this was not a reliable option. So, the other American and I were given an electric scooter to share. Initially, this was a really cool idea; it was summertime, and the idea of commuting to and from the city was an exciting one. I have to say, though, all that excitement went away after the first riding experience. To make a long story short, the scooter simply wasn't powerful enough to haul two hefty American football players at once. Although it was no problem going down the big hill to the main city, going up it proved to be impossible. I remember the scooter stalling halfway up the hill, which meant that we had to play "rock, paper, scissors" for the right to ride the scooter back to Hanfeld, while the other was forced to take the hour-long walk. As two Americans, who were used to driving everywhere, this routine quickly became old for both of us.

Looking back on this situation, these are very minor issues, which could have surely been resolved simply by communicating them to the club. Nevertheless, we chose to take matters into our own hands. Totally fed up with the situation, we both decided that enough was enough; we made up our minds to head home to the States. So, we called the airlines and re-booked our flights, for a month earlier than scheduled. The huge mistake was that we decided we weren't going to tell anybody.

I remember the night before leaving we cleaned the apartment, washed all our football equipment, folded up our game and practice jerseys neatly, and left everything nice and orderly on the kitchen table. I guess this was all an effort to do a good deed, to lighten the blow of our sneaky escape. I remember we even had some extra equipment that we didn't want to haul back with us to the U.S.A., so we left a note telling the club to give the extra equipment to some of the youth players. While that sure felt like a good deed at the time, in hindsight it didn't cover up our immature actions. To put the cherry on top, I remember being at the U-bahn station, waiting for our ride to Munich Airport and realizing that we still had our apartment keys with us. So, we began to debate with one another the best way to deal with the situation: should we just keep the keys, return to Hanfeld to leave them at the apartment, or simply dispose of the evidence? I made the decision to keep my key, while my teammate proceeded toward the nearest trash can and tossed his key inside. "Problem solved," he said. I chuckled as we entered the train, never to see Hanfeld again.

When I returned home to Pittsburgh, I realized that I had made the wrong decision. I did mail the key back to Hanfeld, but after that I essentially shunned all other thoughts of the situation.

Despite the frustrating circumstances which took place in Hanfeld, I refused to take responsibility for my actions. However, after a few years went by and my experiences and maturity continued to grow, I couldn't help but think about my time in Germany, and I knew I had to try and apologize. I reached out to the general manager of the club and told him how sorry I was. He was kind and said that he forgave me.

As good as it felt to finally apologize, while in a way removing a burden I had been carrying, the moral of this story is not to be apologetic; it is to take responsibility for your mistakes, by admitting, accepting and learning from them, becoming a better person as a result.

The decision I made to flee Hanfeld, as an immature 22-year-old, is one that a large majority of young, imported players would have likely made as well. Fleeing from discomfort has become a norm in modern-day society, whether that be dropping out of school because it is too hard, getting a divorce because of too much arguing or outside sexual temptation, or quitting a job because you feel disrespected and underappreciated. The fact of the matter is that true leaders don't flee from discomfort; they learn to thrive in it. This is a lesson I learned through making a huge mistake.

That being said, I admitted, I accepted, I learned and I became a better man from it. To that little town of Hanfeld, Germany, and all the chickens running around, which I once chastised and despised, I now say thank you.

THE TASK: THE SWAL LIFESTYLE

We can be creatures who are prone to double-mindedness. We always want the things that we don't have, or are thinking about how our lives can be better, by only focusing on our negative qualities and situations; this is also commonly described: *"The grass is greener on the other side."* If we are in a relationship, we think about being single and vice-versa; if we are unemployed, we long and pray to find that full-time job to pay the bills, only to figure out that when we do get a job – which is supposed to solve our problems and fulfil us – it actually makes things worse, because we are unhappy with the hours, pay or people we work with. Think of a time where you really, really wanted something. Maybe it was your first car or, as mentioned, a job. Then reflect on the moment you finally had the thing for which you longed. Maybe at first you were in awe and full of joy, but then after a while you start to realize that you could also have more or better, and you turned your desires to something else. This is one example of double-mindedness at its finest.

I must say from experience that double-mindedness is undoubtedly the biggest foe in the pursuit of living the SWAL life. A false narrative exists, that one is only responsible for being a leader while at the office, in the field or in the meeting room; whatever else happens outside of office hours is not seen as important to your status in a leadership role. This couldn't be further from the truth. Part-time leadership (double-mindedness) is a recipe for eventual disaster.

The term double-mindedness is defined as:

"wavering in mind: undecided, vacillating;
marked by hypocrisy: insecure"

Right below that definition, you'll find a reference to the book of *James*, chapter 1, verse 8 in the Bible, which reads:

"...a double minded man, unstable in all his ways."

This verse is one that is so vital to understand. The Bible says that double-mindedness will get us nowhere. We cannot expect to live a double-minded lifestyle as an effective leader; SWAL is a lifestyle in itself. We must accept the necessary sacrifices that most aren't willing to make, and demonstrate it in everything that we do. That means giving up getting wasted at the club until 4 a.m.; not smoking that cigarette or blunt that you know will help you relax after a long day; not "rewarding" yourself with feasting on junk food, after a long, hard week. It means waking up at 5 a.m. if necessary, to get in a workout or prepare for that meeting, game or deadline that is coming up. We must understand that taking on a leadership role means we must live the life of the minority. We become effective leaders because we are built differently internally.

Part of being different is having the ability to fight the urges and temptation of what society sees as enjoyable or satisfying, because in the end those things that are satisfying distract us from our ultimate purpose. This is often a major sticking point in regard to genuine leadership. The vast majority of people want to have the best of both worlds: they want to be part-time (double-minded) leaders without facing the consequences. To put it bluntly, this is a mentality which will ultimately lead to failure. Just as a part-time job only pays you a small portion of money for your output, and simply doesn't pay the bills, double-minded leadership only produces a limited amount of success.

We see this idea of double-minded leadership occurring often in professional sports. As we all know, the lifestyle of a professional athlete is one of temptation and lust. These athletes are being paid astronomical amounts of money for their skills in their respective sport. They are constantly being observed and bombarded by fans in public and on social media. However, despite the temptation from the outside, they are paid to remain grounded and focused on their jobs. Unfortunately, for a lot of them, this isn't always the case; many get caught up in the lavish lifestyle off the field (which often leads to struggles on the field), and credibility issues within the locker room. Referring to the position of quarterback in the N.F.L., in almost every case they are the most highly paid, admired and recognized players on the team; they are often referred to as the "face of the franchise". The problem with this is that with greater status comes greater temptation. Add to this the fact that most of these players are young adults in their early twenties, fresh out of living the college lifestyle; it is so easy for them to lose sight of the fact that they are automatically deemed the leaders of the team and held to a higher standard, as far as maintaining a professional and respectable image goes.

In respect of history, the sports world has seen young, talented quarterbacks (and other professional athletes, for that matter) get consumed by the fame, money, wrong crowd of people, women, alcohol, drugs, problems with the law, and so on. This unfortunately leads many leaders down a dark path, with an extreme uphill battle to climb. Living under a microscope, their every move is calculated and judged by the general public. Some can handle and thrive on this responsibility, while others simply crumble and give in. It is difficult to predict how one will react until they are placed in that situation.

In any case, the moral is for one to understand that the decisions outside of the working environment can and will impact one's persona and perception as a leader within the working environment. As a person in a leadership role, whether we realize it or not, we are always being watched, critiqued, judged and even mimicked. Due to this, we cannot live a double-minded lifestyle, only expecting to be judged when we are in our work setting. Throughout my experiences I have learned that everyone has the capability within to become an effective leader, but not everyone has the will to use that capability to lead effectively. In simpler terms, not everyone can effectively lead because few are willing to accept the responsibility, pressure and lifestyle changes which are necessary.

Double-mindedness also applies to decision-making and direction. Aside from lifestyle choices, double-mindedness has another side to it: the inability to make proper and/or singly-focused decisions. Being indecisive is being destructive. When we aren't able to plan and make decisions with security and confidence, we are setting ourselves and our team back, and we are wasting valuable time which can't be given back.

One may say: "Hey, Zach, I think this is a load of B.S. I see a lot of people in leadership roles who are not adapting to the SWAL lifestyle, who are living double-minded, yet are having loads of success. I can have both, as long as I perform when I am in my working realm." I would respond by warning how deceptive appearances can be, from the outside looking in. Those people who are living a part-time leadership life know deep down inside that they are a fraud. When people with deeply ingrained morals realize they are wrong and they are living a lie, it eats them up inside. At this point, it is only a matter of time until they realize a change for the better is a must – not just for the sake of their credibility, but for their own personal mental health. I know this to be the truth because I lived through the exact situation myself; this led to my emotional rollercoaster and somewhat backwards life journey (hopefully, you will understand what I mean by "backwards" at the end of this summary).

I spent most of my childhood and teenage years with clear goals and aspirations of earning a Division 1 football scholarship, then going on to play for the N.F.L. Most kids who grow up playing football in the U.S.A. have this dream, in one form or another; the difference with me was that I realized early on the distractions which prevented most kids my age from seeing this dream through until the end. I made a personal promise to myself that I would be different, and make the necessary sacrifices to make it happen.

In retrospect, I was probably mature beyond my years, in the sense that I knew that I needed to block out all the noise around me, even if that meant going to extremes. This meant giving up the life of a typical teenage high school student, including going to parties, underage drinking, having a girlfriend(s), or engaging in dangerous/enjoyable activities which would otherwise jeopardize my dream. I had very high expectations for myself, and always judged myself based on my failures and not my successes. I wasn't perfect by any means, and I had my fair share of slip-ups along the way.

What was so disappointing was that, by the time my senior year of high school came around, despite all my sacrifices, I clearly wasn't any closer to my Division 1 football dream. At the time when I should have already made my decision on where I was going to accept my scholarship offer and attend college, I was a 5-foot-8-inch-tall, 170-pound quarterback with no varsity starting experience. I had lost the starting quarterback battle as a junior, and was left with only one year to prove myself, and somehow miraculously keep my dream alive. Despite my stature and lack of experience, I still had faith that I was going to Division 1 and then somehow to the N.F.L. So, to make a long story short, to my disappointment, my one season as the starting quarterback went by rather unimpressively. We ended the season with a 3-6 record, and I had played terribly in the final game of the season, which we needed to win in order to make the playoffs. I was so dejected, because I had put so much work into that off-season, knowing I was going to get the chance to play. When that season ended, part of my passion for the game of football went with it. I began to consider quitting altogether, and pursuing a baseball career in college.

I appreciated hearing people tell me things like: "Zach, you are a great leader and role model"; "You do it the right way"; "You have the toughness to be a Marine one day." While I did truly take pride in these compliments, it all seemed secondary to me. I didn't want to just be known as the tough, gritty, little guy with great leadership qualities; in my mind, this was almost like a back-handed compliment. These were all qualities that people in the football world associated with players who weren't very talented, but tried their best, and were therefore respected. This ate me up inside. I wanted to be known as Zach the great Division 1 quarterback prospect, who was *also* a great leader and role model.

Nevertheless, despite my forgettable high school career, I was able to refocus and find my passion for football again. I accepted an offer to walk on at a Division 2 school. In my naïve mind, I would go there and put up huge numbers, then transfer to a Division 1 school which would offer me a full scholarship. Despite this plan of mine, predictably it didn't go as calculated. After red-shirting (only a practice player) my freshman season and being the number six quarterback on the depth chart, I decided to transfer to a Division 3 school closer to home. I was able to get some starting experience that year, but this was the first time I began to re-think my goals.

I will never forget the night when it all changed. I finally, for the first time in my life since I was five years old, lay in my dorm room in the pitch dark and realized, and accepted, that I was never going to the N.F.L.; the dream I had dedicated my whole life toward was finally over. I began to question why I gave up so much as a child and in high school, only to be left at a small, Division 3 school in the middle of nowhere, playing small-time football while earning an accounting degree. I was on the path to standardized societal norms. My dream of being in the minority was heading straight down the path of the majority.

At this point in time, I was just angry at the world. I decided that I was going to drop out of college and give up football altogether, so that's what I did; I returned home to live with my mom, all while attending community college and working as a city maintenance worker. As unglamorous as this sounds, I just needed to get away from it all, so I ran away from my shortcomings.

It is amazing how God works, because at my lowest moment is when my life drastically changed.

I remember sitting in the living room with my mom, as she described her next trip to Europe. Europe? I asked why she would ever go there.

"I am going to Portugal," she said. "You should think about traveling there one day; it is very beautiful."

I remember laughing and saying: "I am from the best country in the world. There are beautiful places here, as well, so why would I need to go across the ocean to see beauty?"

Despite my animosity and Americanized morals, I couldn't help but remember playing the *Madden N.F.L. Football* video games as a kid in the early 2000s, and seeing teams I didn't recognize: the Rhine Fire, the Hamburg Sea Devils and the Barcelona Dragons. This got me curious. So, after talking to my mom I did a quick Google search and found that, despite the fact that N.F.L. Europe no longer exists, American football (yes, you must specify "American" football in Europe) overseas was actually alive and well. They even had a recruiting website for American players looking to play in Europe. So, just out of curiosity, I created a profile and uploaded some of my brief high school highlights; what could it hurt, right? To my amazement, two days later I got an email from a coach, inquiring about my interest in playing professional football in Poland. Poland?! The only Poland I knew of was Poland, Ohio, because a few of my former college teammates were from there; I knew nothing about "The European Country Poland". At first, I somewhat scoffed at the offer, because it wasn't for a lot of money, and I was making almost triple the offered amount at my construction worker job.

But, to make a long story short, despite backlash from family and friends, I decided that accepting the offer was better than getting a farmer's tan in the hot sun all day, while digging holes and laying concrete. So, within the span of one week, I went from the college football player dropout, who knew nothing about Europe, to a European professional quarterback, on his first international flight to Poland.

I remember saying to myself, as I was on the plane, that I was going to change my mentality. I was going to make up for the lost time and enjoy myself, and all that came with being a professional athlete – despite being paid like a pizza delivery guy. That didn't matter to me; the bottom line was that I was being paid to play the sport I loved – that was enough for me. As a 20-year-old, who had never drunk a sip of alcohol, I was determined to make a change and start enjoying the simpler things in life. From there, I never looked back; I ended up playing seven more years in Europe, in countries such as France, Germany, Italy and Austria. And I can honestly say that it has been the best decision of my life. I loved Europe so much that I now live here full time. There is no doubt that my life was changed for the better.

However, I must say that not all of it was for the better; it is safe to say that the relaxed European lifestyle got to me. Despite having the time of my life in Europe, with a lot of success on the field (and off the field, meeting amazing people and beautiful women), in the long run it got me into a lot of trouble. I had totally changed my identity from the young, determined teen I used to be. I remember coming home to visit my family and friends back in the States, and them telling me that I had changed; that I was different, and that it was a good thing. I was definitely more relaxed, joking and open to having fun. While this sounds all well and good, the reality was that I got trapped in the lifestyle as a professional player in Europe. Basically, I was a 26-year-old guy who had everything he needed to live: I had an apartment, average salary, free time, women and friends – for me, that was all I needed. Yes, I was a so-called team leader/captain of my team, but the term *leadership* had taken on a new and unauthentic meaning. In terms of SWAL, I was a total fraud; I had become a part-time leader. I was going out to the club at the weekends, meeting up with girls rather than watching films or preparing for the next game and, most devastating, avoiding the responsibility of preparing for my post-athletic career. I was so distracted by chasing the life I thought I had missed out on, that I failed to set myself up for when my body failed me, and no team saw value in what I could offer. So that young, 18-year-old kid who was goal-oriented, a role model and great leader, had become a 26-year-old, immature, unmotivated football player with a bad left knee, multiple concussions, no plans or goals, except for being a ladies' man, no savings, fake friends, and a long road ahead to finding his true identity.

Yes, I got the experience I had been looking for – I had, in a sense, made up for the lost time – but as most of my immature friends in high school were getting their lives together, mine was falling apart. I like to refer to this as my (backwards) "Benjamin Button life", referring to the famous movie. In a sense, it seemed as if the older I got, the more unstable and immature I became. For those of you who haven't seen the movie or heard of the disease, please take a minute to stop reading and give it a quick Google search. All of a sudden, I had become exactly what I had been fighting against my whole childhood and teenage life. I felt lost and hopeless.

It wasn't until I took a job coaching a youth football team in Italy that I finally began to see the light again. As I began to work with these kids, it was clear to me that they needed guidance; a lot of them didn't have big brothers or father figures in their lives, to help lead them down the right path. After spending more and more time with these kids, I began to realize my purpose again. God had never intended for me to become an N.F.L. football player – however, He let me chase that dream in Europe, in order to find myself and my true purpose: to inspire young people.

For about a three-year period, I lived a selfish lifestyle, leaning on my status as an American professional quarterback in Europe to justify my role as a leader. In reality, I was a fraud: double-minded, selfish as could be and living a lie. During these times, I would think about all the fun I had been having, as a way of self-reassurance that I was doing the right thing. Nevertheless, as the trials and tribulations began to add up, and as my body began to fail me, I developed more and more mental health issues. I am just so thankful for the discovery of youth football coaching. These kids helped keep me grounded, and inspired me to take action to rebuild my life and become an effective leader once again.

Like most of us, I am still fighting every day; I am still not where I need to be. I know I have dug myself into a big hole living this Benjamin Button lifestyle, but I have no other choice but to fight and trust that God is leading me on a path toward becoming the best version of myself.

Why do I tell you this story? Not because I expect you to care about my life, and the trials and tribulations I have gone through; I realize that we all have our own issues, which we are forced to deal with on a daily basis. I tell you this because I want you to realize that part-time leadership and double-mindedness will eventually expose your flaws, internally and externally. There simply is no way to lead effectively as a part-time leader. Whether it happens from within your own mind, or is evident to society, double-mindedness will expose you at your worst, in one way or another.

We all have to sit back and decide if we want to truthfully take on this lifestyle of SWAL. Like my former self, I have come to realize the reality that the decision to adapt to the SWAL lifestyle is one that most aren't willing to make. I also know that there are and will be times in everyone's life when we question the life we are living. Thoughts that will come to mind are ones of purpose, credibility and whether one's life is one of success and self-control, or one of failure, fraud and recklessness.

I have also realized that one of the hardest thoughts to control is the one that we are "missing out" on all the world has to offer. Most people would assess SWAL and realize that accepting it means to lose out on various experiences the world portrays as fun or enjoyable. That is a fair assumption, if those aspects are of your utmost importance. Yet, trust me when I tell you that you are not missing out. Despite some short-term pleasure from living a life the world perceives as gratifying, most people who seem to be having the time of their life (while hiding the fact that they rely on their job title or bank account to justify their leadership status) are often the ones who are the emptiest and most mentally unstable behind closed doors. I tell you this because I was one of those people.

So, set clear goals, don't get caught up in being double-minded, discover or rediscover your passion as the leader for your own SWAL life, surround yourself with quality mentors and commit to a lifestyle of effective leadership, despite worldly temptation. This is not to say that it isn't okay to have fun every once in a while; the key is to understand the fine line between innocent fun and self-destructiveness. Making these decisions comes down to choice, commitment, action and facing fears. If you truly want to have an impact, understand that you must live the life of the minority. It is not for everyone, and most will choose to go against it; but for people who strive for greatness, impact and a lasting legacy, SWAL is the answer.

THE CHALLENGE: IF YOU DON'T USE IT, YOU LOSE IT

There is a story in the Bible, located in *Matthew* 25:14-30, called "The Parable of the Talents". In this story, Jesus describes a rich man and his three slaves. The man gives each slave some money, in the Greek unit of currency known as a "talent" (worth about 6,000 denari; several thousand dollars by today's standards); he gives his first slave five talents, the second two talents and the third only one. The master told his servants that he would be leaving on a journey, and that they should take care of his money while he was gone; he told them he would return and evaluate them on how they handled these talents. The master eventually returned and found that the first two servants had invested wisely, and were able to double their talents; he told them: "Well done!" However, when he asked the third servant about his one talent, the servant responded that he hid it from danger, so it would not get stolen or harmed. The master then scolded him, proclaiming that he should have invested his talent like the others, in order to build more talents.

Believe it or not, this story relates to the application of SWAL. As aspiring leaders, we must take the time to use and enhance our talents, which stem from our personal foundation (tools). Otherwise, we become lazy and content like the third servant, causing us to lose our talents and credibility altogether. We must take time for personal development, and understand when to bring out our tools, and which situation calls for them. This is the purpose of SWAL: we have to understand the tools we have within our personal foundation, then understand the tools we need to use in each specific situation. The ability to understand which tools need to be used at which time is a tool in itself. This comes through experience and taking time to hone one's craft and build on these talents, rather than burying them. The ability to grow and develop our skills is something that can make the difference in our longevity as an effective leader.

THE ULTIMATE CHALLENGE: LEADING WHILE LOSING

As competitors, we all want to win. Whether that be in a game of chess against our grandfather, a race against our big brother, competition for a new job or anything else; we all desire success.

Despite the fact that we all enjoy winning in every aspect of life, more often than not there are times when we lose and lose hard. Failure is the ultimate test of a true leader.

Leadership roles are given for how we handle adversity or failure. Think about that for a minute. Why do we have presidents, C.E.O.s, captains, head coaches and managers? It is not to stand at a podium and smile because everything is great; their positions exist because they are trusted to best guide their following through tough times and losses.

Let me tell you a story about a time in my life where this concept was truly put to the test. It was during the summer of 2016, in Naples, Italy. I had just lost my current job and recently accepted the head coaching job for a team called the Napoli 82ers. At the time I was homeless, living with a coach of mine, and I didn't have enough money to rent a new apartment – therefore, I would commonly use public laundry services, just down the street from my coach's place. Even though I was living on pasta and espressos, I was thankful that I at least had enough clothes that I didn't need to worry. That was until one day, when I hung my clothes out to dry and went for a walk around the city (which I did every time I laundered); I returned to an empty clothesline. Yes, all my clothes had been stolen! So now I was homeless, surviving on $650 a month, a pasta and coffee diet and nothing but the clothes on my back. Additionally, I was expected to meet my new players and give an opening speech the very next day; talk about leading while losing! Life had me by the throat, and I could have very easily called my family back in the States and told them to book me a flight home; I could have quit right then, and returned home to a warm bed and all the necessities I needed. I can't tell you how close I was to making that call. However, the next day at the players' meeting, I saw the look of joy and determination in their eyes, as I preached to them how we were going to do many great things together, and how I would take them to where they wanted to be, as long as they followed my lead. Ironically, I was a nervous wreck who didn't even have a spare T-shirt (thank God Naples is in the south of Italy). Nevertheless, those players gave me hope and helped me realize that this was about more than just myself. Despite all my shortcomings, I knew that I needed to show strength, and do everything in my power to effectively lead them.

I made a choice that day to lead while losing, and I can tell you I am damn proud of it. In sports, one thing I have come to realize is that winning tends to cover up for a lot of issues going on behind the scenes, which would otherwise end disastrously. When your team wins, leadership is easy; you will be praised, unquestioned, patted on the back and maybe even given a raise. However, when you start to lose is when the real test comes into play. And, let me tell you, the difference between winning and losing is a matter of seconds, inches and brief moments; oftentimes, the difference between being considered the best in your field and being fired is a matter of a simple, lucky break. This is why we as aspiring leaders must be prepared to lose.

This may sound like a negative statement, but it is a simple fact. We have to adopt the mentality of preparing and expecting to win, while preparing to lead effectively while losing, as well. Essentially, we prepare for every outcome (win or lose), but expect one thing (to win); we do not expect to lose, but we must prepare for it, because adversity will come. One of the biggest mistakes a person can make in a leadership role is to be naïve and negligent toward failure; if one chooses to rely solely on winning and current states of comfort, he is playing a dangerous game. Aspiring leaders must accept that failure will eventually occur, in one way or another. The way you carry yourself and guide your followers through the tough times will carry much more weight than when you guide them through the glory days; this is when being a leader is easy. The best leaders stay calm and navigate the storm. Think of a captain on a large ship at sea: sure, when the weather is great and the sun is out, he and his crew can sit back and take in the fresh air, while cruising along to their destination; however, what will he do when the inevitable storm hits? What will he do when suddenly that peaceful ride turns into one of hellish proportions? The truth is, he will never know until he experiences it himself, just like you, as aspiring leaders, will not know how you will handle losing until you are faced with it.

These moments, and how you handle them, will ultimately decide your fate and credibility in a leadership role. The way you handle the difficult times will be how you are judged and perceived amongst your following. Figuratively speaking, we have to prepare for the storm ahead, and understand that we must be the calm within the storm. These storms may come in all shapes and sizes: some are brief and intense, others long and intense; some are brief and minor, and others still are long but minor. Nevertheless, I cannot stress enough that aspiring leaders must understand the importance of them all. These are the times when we can refer back to SWAL and our personal foundation tools, in order to navigate these storms to calmer waters.

HARD FACTS: HARD WORK GUARANTEES NOTHING

Hard work pays off. How many times have we heard these four words throughout our lives? Whether from our parents, teachers, coaches or mentors, the idea of hard work has been pounded into our brains since childhood.

Well, let me point out the elephant in the room on this one…

So many people preach about hard work, and the idea that working hard is the answer to all problems. For example, when an athlete wins an Olympic medal and, in the interview afterward, the reporter asks, "How did you do it?", the classic answer is usually something like, "A lot of hard work and dedication." So, you mean to tell me that the person who finished fourth without a medal didn't work hard and dedicate himself? Of course he did. The fact of the matter is that, more often than not, our hard work will not pay off in the way we anticipate.

Hard work guarantees nothing. It doesn't even guarantee an opportunity for results. We as leaders have to understand that. When push comes to shove, the only thing that hard work guarantees is personal discipline and the development of quality habits; by working hard, we train our brain to become more disciplined and focused, rather than having an insecure mindset with no real plans or goals.

Now, I know this idea may seem like a bit of a let-down to most people – after all, we have always been told that hard work is the key to success. However, there is a secret reason for working hard. This reason is based on the personal discipline resulting from our hard work. This self-discipline is a major contributor toward effective leadership development. If we can discipline ourselves to push through the hard times, when things aren't going our way, we will be in a better position to have success in the future. Without personal discipline, leaders have no credibility, and tend to quit when times get tough. If you take the time to learn about the successful people in this world, there is one quality that you find common to all of them: they all possess relentless self-discipline. They all had the ability to restrain themselves and focus on their goals, while avoiding outside temptations, criticisms or distractions.

Now, I will say there is a way to have our hard work translate directly into success. How is this done? Simply put, we have to focus on the direction of the hard work, in direct correlation to our goals and aspirations. We need to make sure that there is no wasted effort in the work we are putting in. Efficiency is the key to expedited results.

Many people will tell you that, if you put in the time, then the results will follow. Despite this widely used approach, seldom is it ever proven to be the truth. This is because we as individuals often make three major mistakes in regard to our efforts: the first mistake is that we lack focus in key areas, aside from the obvious. For example, a lot of people want to get in shape nowadays: in today's "fitness boom", people are going to the gym more now than at any point in history. It is one thing to go to the gym and work hard during your workouts; however, without a healthy diet to complement this hard physical work, one will rarely experience any type of positive physical changes to his or her body. This often causes frustration, and many people tend to give up at this point. They fail to understand the importance of a healthy diet, in cooperation with physically training their bodies, in order to maximize success. This lack of knowledge, willingness or priority put into one's diet leads to wasted effort in the gym.

The second mistake we make is that we try to reinvent the wheel in whatever we are trying to accomplish. Everyone nowadays wants to be an innovator and do things their way. This is not a bad mentality, by any stretch of the imagination; however, this methodology can also lead to dead ends, due to a lack of information or historical references to learn from. Think about a chemist, who spends hours in his lab trying to invent a method to clone humans: he spends hours upon hours in his lab, slaving away on his whiteboard, mapping out various equations, examining molecules and totally investing his life's work into finding a solution for cloning – unfortunately, he has no proven formula or leads to go by; never in the history of mankind has someone successfully cloned a human being. Our chemist is participating in what I like to call "the Blind Grind": the Blind Grind refers to working hard at something, with no clear ideas or assurances that your hard work is substantially contributing to any goal or hoped-for outcome. This can be a very frustrating place to be for an individual.

There have been many times in my life when I have put a lot of time and effort into things, with no idea how they would turn out. For example, I once decided to start a food vending business in Salzburg, Austria. Being an American citizen, my plan was to sell Americanized, healthy protein-packed snacks, for people looking to get fit. I spent hours coming up with a PowerPoint presentation, to pitch to investors at the local shopping malls and gyms, along with creating a business plan and logo for the company. I was feeling great about all the work I had put in. Ironically, it didn't even cross my mind to consider whether or not this was something that people would actually be interested in, and it turned out that there was little to no interest. Firstly, Salzburg, Austria is a small city, and there weren't enough shopping malls or gyms to target. Also, I didn't take into account the start-up costs, laws, regulations and differing tax structure when planning to start a business in Austria; I quickly found that there was a lot more to it than I had initially considered. So, it is safe to say that my innovative idea did not reap the benefits of my hard work. What I should have done is to have researched the market in Salzburg and found a niche where there was a need, or track record of success. Then, I could have taken that need and worked hard to become the best provider of that particular service or product. However, my innovative mindset played to my disadvantage in this case, and a lot of time was lost in the end.

The last, most common and most detrimental mistake most people make is that they do not make a decision. This goes back to the trap of double-mindedness I mentioned earlier. A lot of people have insecurities about what they truly want to do, or what is truly their purpose, and I am no exception to this tendency; there are times when I have sat back and thought about my current path, and questioned whether that was the path I truly wanted to pursue. Double-mindedness is the ultimate paralyzer of action and potential success.

Many people confuse the concept of double-mindedness with open-mindedness. There is a huge difference: double-mindedness leads to spurts of unstructured hard work in a variety of potential areas, without ever finishing or following through with any type of impactful action. How many of you have decided to do something or take on an endeavor but, for whatever reason, you changed your mind halfway through, or let others' opinions focus your attention elsewhere? Then, you begin some new venture and the cycle repeats itself: one's lack of commitment leads to dead ends. Focused commitment and hard work must be in sync with one another, in order to achieve success. Without making a commitment to a single goal, our hard work turns into double-mindedness, and wasted time and effort.

The Bible says, in *James*, chapter 1, verses 7-8:

"That person should not expect to receive anything from the LORD. Such a person is double-minded and unstable in all they do."

These two verses say it all, in my opinion. One who is uncommitted or indecisive should expect no progress or reward for their efforts. Yet, we as a society preach that hard work will always lead to results. As a result of this misleading mantra, when people do work hard and don't get the results they want, most give up or lose hope. We as SWALeaders need to realize that double-mindedness is a real issue which often goes unnoticed, due to society's flawed idea of success (just work hard in whatever, and you will be successful).

Not only is this a recipe for failure, but it is also an extreme waste of your most valuable asset, time. Efficient, dynamic leaders are also efficient time managers. Every moment of time is highly regarded and geared toward goal achievement. Simply put, zero wasted time and effort equals maximum effective results. Speaking from personal experience, I can't tell you the amount of time I have wasted simply due to the fact that I did not commit it toward a specific goal. I admit, I am likely more guilty of being double-minded than anyone. That said, those who can realize this trap will be much better off in regard to their levels of success, and the timeframe in which that success occurs. The irony is that double-mindedness is often detected by people from the outside, but rarely is realized from within.

People who are double-minded are not capable of making confident decisions. They are always jumping from one project/idea to another, always with a justification for their erratic behavior. They rationalize with themselves as to why their original idea wasn't the right one, find ways to compensate and make excuses for why they can't finish a given project.

Once again, it is so important to harp on the danger of double-mindedness, and the role it plays in one's inability to maintain credibility and progressive leadership development. When in doubt, make a decision, do your research and focus all action toward that decision, while ignoring the noise around you.

TIP OF THE CAP: HANG YOUR HAT

"Hanging your hat", by my definition, is the idea that you have one or two characteristics/skills within yourself that you consider of high importance, and with which you strongly identify. These aspects will allow you to always have a sense of pride and comfort, knowing that you have proven skill(s) to fall back on, especially when times are tough. These "hat-hangers" will also help you maintain credibility and give your following a feeling of assurance. Hat-hangers also go a long way in shaping our personal identity, knowing that no matter what happens, these traits are there for us to lean on.

For example, I consider my faith and fitness my hat-hangers. There have been times in my life when I have let people down, lost my focus, been fired from a job, been financially broke without a home, been chastised by my peers and so on. In these difficult times, without my faith and fitness to keep me grounded, I could have very easily lost my identity; I would have likely taken a sudden turn for the worse. I used my love of training and my faith in God to push me through those difficult times. I knew that, in the end, despite my situation, I had to maintain my identity as a physically fit young man, who had faith that God had his best interest in mind.

This is similar to the concept of SWAL, in the sense of one's personal foundation. It is important not to confuse our "hat hangers" with the tools within our personal foundation, in respect to SWAL; there is a distinct difference. Hat-hangers are specific, personal, elite-level qualities which each and every individual possesses. These are qualities we use to help shape our identity and lead ourselves. On the contrary, the tools within our personal foundation are skills that we develop, in order to lead others in the most effective way. Hat-hangers give us comfort, knowing that no matter how dire our situation gets, we always have one or two elite qualities, which can be tapped into at any time, due to their ingrained importance. Even more notably, they give us a sense of pride and self-confidence, when times are at their worst.

One may ask, how does a person acquire hat-hangers? I have come to realize that they are acquired through passion, ability and importance. For example, let's imagine that your passion is writing poetry in your free time. Due to this passion, you see poetry as an important practice in regard to your identity. As time goes by, and passion and importance grow, these qualities eventually turn into abilities (hat-hangers), via focused action. With passion and ability comes importance.

It is also important to know that the aspects of passion, ability and importance (the priority placed on developing a skill) are all interchangeable. After passion, importance and focused action are implemented, you have unintentionally created your own personal hat-hanger. As I stated earlier, one of my hat-hangers is my faith; one Bible verse that I hang my hat on deals with feelings of fear. We, as aspiring leaders and human beings, all have to deal with fear at one point or another. This could be anything from the first time we lead a project or team to being diagnosed with a serious illness. Fear and nerves play a role in our lives, whether we want to admit it or not. That being said, according to *Isaiah*, chapter 41, verse 10, we can find our peace in these times of fear. It states:

> *"So do not fear, for I am with you; do not be dismayed, for I am your God. I will strengthen you and help you; I will uphold you with my righteous right hand."*

As leaders, this verse can be so comforting to those who are believers.

It helps us understand that, no matter what we go through, and no matter how much fear we face, we will be strengthened by God if we choose to take refuge in His presence. This is a verse that I often look back on, due to the calming peace it offers. It has supported me during my trials and tribulations, not only in my various leadership roles, but in everyday life encounters.

RULE OF THUMB: TRUST YOUR GUT

Previously, I stated and explained how aspiring SWALeaders need to avoid making "blind" decisions; instead, they should make decisions based on clear observations and analysis. Though I am not backing down from this statement by any means, I also believe there are times when there are exceptions to this rule – by "exception", I mean those situations where the maintenance of our morals is at stake. In these tense situations, our best option is to trust our gut instinct.

All of us have had a "gut feeling" (good or bad), at one point or another in our lives. These feelings are often controversial, because they sometimes do not make sense when we are experiencing them; maybe all of the data and our analysis is telling us one thing, but in our gut we feel strongly against that data, because our morals as a SWALeader are being challenged. The tricky part about trusting our gut is that it is often hard to justify our decisions to others, who see things strictly as black and white. As people in leadership positions, gut-based decisions are often very controversial, because we are making decisions that don't make a lot of sense to the group, yet they often carry with them a large impact on the group. That being said, if our gut-based decisions turn out to be the incorrect ones, it would be tough to justify the decision to others in a way they would understand.

However, let me give an example of where this concept could come into play in a leadership role. As a coach, I once had a player who was far and away the most physically talented on the team. He was a good looking, fit guy, who was blessed with the abilities of strength, power and speed. Due to his presence and ability the other guys on the team naturally navigated toward him, and he clearly had a strong influence on the other players; you just saw how they reacted when he showed up to the field. It was clear that he had a persona about him that drew others. However, his character was far from a positive one. While his talents on the field were unmatched, his ability to effectively lead was non-existent. He had a selfish attitude, cocky as they come, and a lack of work ethic. In any case, it was clear that the rest of the players looked up to him, due to his on-field success. This wasn't exactly a bad thing at the time, because the team was winning and I was technically doing my job as a coach. Still, I sensed in my gut that something wasn't morally right about the whole situation; it was clear that the attitude of this player was trickling down to the rest of the team. And who could blame them: they were winning! Nevertheless, I noticed that the more we won, the worse his attitude and antics would get; it was almost as if he knew that he was the main reason we were winning, so therefore he could just do whatever he wanted.

In retrospect, I do not blame the young man – after all, he was only nineteen and he definitely was our best player; it is totally understandable to react to success the way he did. That being said, there came a point in time when his behavior became unacceptable. This included showing up late to practice (or not at all), yelling at and chastising teammates, shunning teammates who weren't the best players, forming groups within the team and being divisive – basically, all the things that make a coach's stomach churn. Therefore, I made the decision to bench him for the following game. Now, this was really an easy decision, due to my gut feeling and SWAL mindset; however, it was also a tough decision given my job status. I had to somehow rationally explain to my boss and the president of the club (who was never at practice and never saw these antics) that this was the best decision in the long run for the team. This was a huge risk on my part, in respect of putting my job on the line, not to mention my already insecure financial situation. All the data on the field told me to shut my mouth and turn a blind eye to his antics. Still, my gut told me that what was currently going on was not ethically acceptable; the longer these antics went on, the more likely the team would be destroyed from within, in the long run. Nevertheless, we played the next game without him and (thank God) we actually won. I have to admit that I was definitely anxious the night before, and I don't really want to guess what would have happened if we had lost; let's just say I was already updating my C.V. and scanning various job portals.

The point of this story is: use your instincts of right and wrong, and rely on your personal foundation to override any reasoning related to physical success.

This is a statement that I know will receive a lot of backlash, based on the way our society operates, and the desire to win at all costs. But, don't forget, SWALeadership operates on the idea of having inner peace, knowing that moral values are placed over immoral production or success. Many claim this approach, but very few follow through with it. Too often, nowadays, people are solely focused on results, and will do anything in order to achieve them. I believe that behind every job description and title is also an unwritten responsibility of morality. Many people in leadership positions get so caught up in their job title, in our immediate-results-based society, that they easily forget the importance of being a role model, who stands up against injustice before all else. I understand, more often than not, that our job status depends on us keeping our mouths shut and shunning immoral behavior in times of success; however, as aspiring leaders, we have to understand that those avoidances will sooner or later come back to haunt us. SWALeaders believe that erratic and unethical behavior must be eliminated, above all else. One of the most important lessons I have learned, throughout my life, is that one will never be wrong in the eyes of God, when trusting in and standing up for morality. Once one makes that decision, he or she can be at peace with whatever results come afterward.

These types of decisions require rare choices and traits. That is why being a SWALeader is hard to live by. What we have to remember is that even though gut decisions may sometimes backfire, being an ethically competent individual won't allow us to experience failure for long. As SWALeaders, we must trust our gut and our personal foundation in these types of situations, with the understanding that immoral success will lead to eventual self-destruction.

I want to quickly refer back to this story, with my football team in Naples and our best player, whom I had benched. Unfortunately, he ended up quitting the team. We went on to finish the season with an average record, barely missing the playoffs. I was quite upset that he decided to quit, because I knew that, deep down, he was a good-hearted young man. Nevertheless, that season ended up being my last with the team.

It wasn't until two years later, when I returned to Naples for a visit, that I would see him again. We had a small reunion with all of my players, outside our old practice field, and there he was, now a little bit taller and a little bit more mature, with some facial hair. I was happily surprised that he happened to show up, and we began to talk. He had permanently stopped playing football due to academic demands, but I could see that he had finally realized the point of my decision two years earlier. He didn't say much about it, but when we said our goodbyes he gave me a hug and said: "Grazie, Coach." I am not really sure what changed his perception, but it was clear that he finally saw the big picture. I often looked back at that situation and wondered if I had truly made the right decision for my team; it wasn't until two years later, upon hearing his words, that I was finally convinced that I had.

IF YOU ARE READY: TIME TO GET SWAL

I hope the concept of SWAL, and the personal experiences that I have shared throughout this book, have given you a better understanding of how effective leadership works in today's world. I also hope you had a few laughs along the way.

I want to use this last chapter to describe the last year and a half of my life. I have actually taken a long hiatus from writing, due to a relatively long bout of insecurity and unhappiness. I became a victim of societal norms, by focusing and ruminating over negative thoughts and my finances; I have admittedly fallen away from the SWAL lifestyle that I have been preaching to you all during the course of this entire book. This isn't meant to be a pity party, by any means; I know that I am not the only one who has gone through these lapses.

There are times in life when we will fall off our path. Whether it be the loss of a family member, a scary health diagnosis, seasonal depression or anything else, for that matter, it is important for us all to understand that, regardless of our status, adversity plays no favorites.

One of the most important facets of being a SWALeader is how hard we are willing to fight, to overcome the internal mental battle within all of us. Our long-term success will be defined by how we dig ourselves out of the various holes life will surely dig for us. Nonetheless, with the demands of today's societal norms, it has become an expectation that people in leadership roles are not allowed to outwardly show human emotion and vulnerability. But life doesn't work that way; the game of life plays no favorites, and it doesn't care about what labels civilization places on us. That being said, part of living with the SWAL mindset is understanding that it is okay to be vulnerable sometimes in a leadership role; these vulnerable moments in our lives are our chance to grow stronger.

I can promise you this: the biggest battle we will fight in life will be the one within ourselves. Once we can slay that dragon inside our own minds, the rest of the battle just isn't that difficult anymore. I referenced various Bible verses throughout this book, because I believe that battle is only won by accepting that we can't fight it on our own. I am not saying that any particular religion is correct – in fact, I shy away from the idea of religion, due to its divisive nature; even so, I have learned that if we can approach our lives with a trust that God has our back, no matter what, it is so much easier to be at peace when the struggles of life come upon us. I believe that a person who leads by way of godly principles is a person who gives himself the best chance to sufficiently lead his own life, and subsequently lead others around him. I also understand that everyone has a different relationship (or lack thereof) with God.

This book is not meant to say that people who don't believe in God are not capable of being effective leaders. To be clear, I am simply testifying to what I believe, and what the basis behind SWAL is all about. I am not here to judge, but to justify based on my experiences. As I stated at the beginning of this book, before we can lead others, we must be able to lead ourselves. It all starts from within.

So, I challenge all of you out there, who are going through pain, to keep fighting. Understand that being a SWAL leader means being driven by adversity, not hindered by it. Despite any adversity or intrusive thoughts going on in your mind, be determined to overcome and understand that you are not your thoughts. Allow that adversity in your life to drive you in the direction of becoming a better version of yourself. As you navigate through this process, I am confident that you will naturally begin to adopt the diverse personal foundation necessary for SWAL. You will soon be able to connect with people on another level, because of your understanding that there are others going through pain as well.

I'd like to leave you all with a passage from the late, great Kobe Bryant, from an interview he took part in not long before his sudden passing. Kobe says:

"I think the definition of greatness is to inspire the people next to you. It's how you can inspire a person to then, in turn, inspire another person, [who] then inspires another person. And that's how you create something, I think, [that] lasts forever. And I think that's our challenge as people: to figure out how our story can impact others and motivate them in a way to create their own greatness."

This is what the SWAL concept is all about. The "greatness" Kobe speaks about is the legacy you leave behind for others to continue. Although Kobe passed away all too soon, he left a legacy of greatness behind, for all of us to follow. While I certainly cannot relate to the life of Kobe Bryant, and the fame and success he experienced, I like to believe that I can relate to the growth he experienced throughout his life and professional career, within a leadership role.

At the memorial service for Kobe, his daughter Gianna and the seven others who were lost, his former teammate Shaquille "Shaq" O'Neal told a story about Kobe, from the beginning of his career. Basically, the other players on the team were frustrated because Kobe wasn't passing them the ball during games. Therefore, Shaq met with Kobe and said to him: "Kobe, there is no 'I' in 'team'." Kobe responded: "I know, but there is a 'ME' in that mother-[expletive]." The crowd laughed.

Why do I mention this story? Because I believe this moment, along with the passage before, show the growth of Kobe's leadership, as his life and career went on. He clearly began to see the big picture as he grew older. His skills and ability were never in question; he was undoubtedly the best basketball player every time he stepped onto the court. What he learned, as his career went on, was just how much of an impact he could have outside of basketball. In turn, he was able to expand his greatness well beyond his accomplishments on the court.

That's what it is all about. Nobody is perfect; we will all make mistakes, but the key is to grow from those mistakes and experiences, in order to realize that our legacy is at stake.

Let us, as aspiring leaders, never forget the words and life of Kobe Bryant. His sudden death was a shock and heartbreak, not only to sports fans, but to the entire world's population. Let Kobe be an example and wake-up call to all of us. Life is short and worldly successes don't last, but legacies do; the legacy of Kobe Bryant lives on forever. May we, as aspiring leaders, use Kobe as our role model, as we proceed through life and our quest to leave a lasting legacy.

My hope is that this book helped you realize that the world is in desperate need of quality leadership. We need people who will appreciate the fact that everyone is different, and must be treated as such. I hope that now your life and outlook on leadership have been transformed for the better. When in doubt, choose to be someone's shining light in their darkest hour, and you will never go wrong.

In closing, I encourage you not to run from pain, but embrace it with faith, because on the other side of your pain lies your legacy. God bless you all, and I hope that each and every one of you is able to find the good life as a SWALeader.

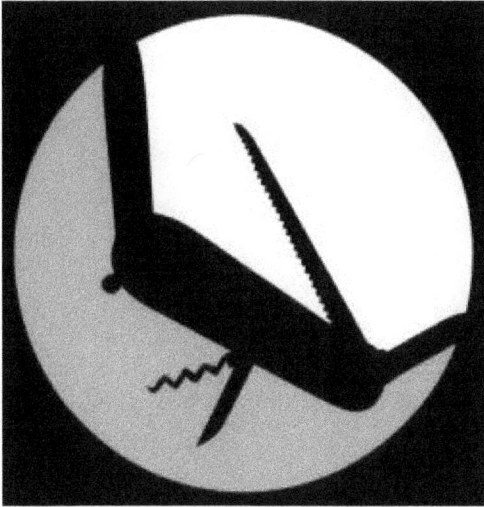

Please follow the *Culture2Culture Blog*:
https://swaleadership.org/blog/

Please "like" and "follow" the Swiss Army Leadership *Facebook* page:
https://www.facebook.com/swaleadership/

You can contact me at:
zach.swaleadership@gmail.com

ACKNOWLEDGEMENTS

Special thanks and appreciation to Chuck Gohn, for all his help and support.

The publisher would like to thank Russell Spencer, Matt Vidler, Laura-Jayne Humphrey, Lianne Bailey-Woodward, Leonard West and Susan Woodard for their hard work and efforts in bringing this book to publication.

ABOUT THE PUBLISHER

L.R. Price Publications is dedicated to publishing books by unknown authors.

We use a mixture of both traditional and modern publishing options, to bring our authors' words to the wider world.

We print, publish, distribute and market books in a variety of formats including paper and hardback, electronic books, digital audiobooks and online.

If you are an author interested in getting your book published, or a book retailer interested in selling our books, please contact us.

www.lrpricepublications.com

L.R. Price Publications Ltd,
27 Old Gloucester Street,
London, WC1N 3AX.
020 3051 9572
publishing@lrprice.com

www.ingramcontent.com/pod-product-compliance
Lightning Source LLC
Chambersburg PA
CBHW071604200326
41519CB00021BB/6868